GREAT PASSENGER SHIPS
1950–1960

GREAT PASSENGER SHIPS
1950–1960

WILLIAM H. MILLER

The History Press

Among the new additions to the worldwide liner fleet in the late 1950s was North German Lloyd's rebuilt *Bremen* (top), the former French *Pasteur*, dating from 1939. During her maiden arrival at New York on a July morning in 1959, she passes another Lloyd liner, the outbound *Berlin*, the former *Gripsholm*, dating from 1925. (North German Lloyd)

Frontispiece: Highlight of the 1950s: the brilliant *United States* departs from New York on its record-breaking maiden voyage, on 3 July 1952. (ALF collection)

Cover illustrations. Front: Painting of the *Rotterdam* by Stephen Card.
Back: Liners at Genoa, 1955. (ALF Collection)

First published 2016

The History Press
The Mill, Brimscombe Port
Stroud, Gloucestershire, GL5 2QG
www.thehistorypress.co.uk

British Library Cataloguing in Publication Data.
A catalogue record for this book is available from the British Library.

ISBN 978 0 7509 6307 7

Typesetting and origination by The History Press
Printed in China

CONTENTS

FOREWORD

Back in the 1950s, in the golden age of the great ocean liners, Cunard Line's *Caronia* was often said to be one of the most luxurious if not the most luxurious liner afloat. She did almost nothing but long, sumptuous and very expensive cruises – around the world, all of the Mediterranean and, in summer, to just about all of Scandinavia. Some 600 crew, many of them handpicked, looked after 600 passengers and so the service ratio was 1:1. A big liner in her own right, the *Caronia* was said to be like a big, floating country club – some passengers actually lived aboard for months at a time. One lady stayed for two years, another for three years and one, the all-time champ of cruising, 'lived' aboard for fourteen years! Painted in shades of green, the *Caronia* was dubbed the 'Green Goddess' – and also called the 'millionaires' yacht'.

I joined the great Cunard Company in 1958 and was promptly assigned to the *Caronia*. I was a junior engineer. The *Caronia* was a plum assignment at Cunard in those days because she travelled just about all over the world. To the hotel staff, the stewards and the waiters, she was much preferred over the other Cunarders, including the legendary *Queen Mary* and *Queen Elizabeth*, because the tips were so much greater. Fifteen-year-old bellboys were given $5 and $10 tips just for opening a door. They did very well. At the dining room entrance, two of them stood to attention and greeted the guests. One would whisper a happy birthday to the other and, upon overhearing this, the passengers might hand him a $50 bill as a present. It was all a sham, of course.

The longest cruises aboard the *Caronia* were the world cruises, with some as long as 108 days. The *Caronia* was created especially as an 'export ship', to bring US dollars into post-war Britain. The great majority of her passengers were older, richer Americans. These very wealthy passengers would come aboard in New York and stay for four months and sometimes longer. Sometimes, Cunard would redecorate their suites to the guests' personal tastes. One lady liked African decor with leopard and zebra skins. The ship's photographer would photograph the suite first so it could later be returned to its original style and decor. I remember Miss McBeth, who stayed aboard for fourteen years, and traveled with a companion. She was rarely seen outside her suite, however. She was a great recluse. But occasionally, she might be seen on the Promenade Deck. On these long cruises, we would sometimes have long stays in port: three or four days in Cape Town, a week in India, four days in Hong Kong. We also had lots of overland tours; some passengers would leave the ship in, say, Bombay and not return until Singapore. Over the years, the crew made friends in the ports of call. Some created businesses – they'd buy jewels in, for example, Rio and then sell them in South Africa. They made great profits!

Barrie Beavis
Summer 2015

ACKNOWLEDGEMENTS

As I've so often said: it takes many hands – like the crew of a big liner – to create such a book. Much appreciation is due. Any and all omissions are deeply regretted. First and foremost my thanks to The History Press and Amy Rigg for taking on this project – and to the editors; special thanks to Stephen Card for the glorious covers; and to Marianne Florio for her foreword.

First-class thanks also to Tom Cassidy, Richard Faber, Michael Hadgis, Norman Knebel, Anthony La Forgia and Captain James McNamara.

Added appreciation to Bill Anunsen, the late Frank Braynard, Captain Nick Carlton, Jim Clench, Anthony Cooke, Irene De Leonardis, the late Alex Duncan, Maurizio Eliseo, Michael Gallagher, Aviva Greenberg, Peter Knego, Herb Maletz, Larry Miller, Tim Noble, Hisashi Noma, Michael Stephen Peters, Peter Plowman, Tony Ralph, the late Antonio Scrimali, Captain Hans van Biljouw and the late Everett Viez.

Companies and organisations that have assisted include: Bethlehem Steel Corporation, Costa Line, Cunard Line, Flying Camera Inc., Holland America Line, Italian Line, Moore-McCormack Lines, Moran Towing & Transportation Company, National Geographic Society, North German Lloyd, Pacific Steam Navigation Co. Ltd, Photofest, Port Authority of New York & New Jersey, Swedish American Line, Steamship Historical Society of America, United States Lines, World Ocean & Cruise Liner Society, World Ship Society and Zim Lines.

INTRODUCTION

When the Second World War ended completely in the summer of 1945 with the Japanese surrender, the world looked to tomorrow – to peace, to the future, to rebuilding, to a new age. In shipping, the losses had been staggering: 50 per cent of the passenger ships present in 1939 were gone, either destroyed or kept for government or further military service. Rebuilding was certainly the order of the day. The future meant, after all, the resumption of commercial services – and not only on the famed transatlantic run, but also to South America, Africa, the Far East and, with huge numbers of migrants, to Australia. Indeed, busy days were ahead.

On the North Atlantic, there were some new if at first moderately sized ships such as the 11,700-ton, 395-passenger *Stockholm* and the 250-bed, all first-class *Media* and *Parthia*. Perhaps the most luxurious and certainly largest, however, in the immediate post-war period was Cunard's sumptuous *Caronia* – 34,000 tons and fitted for just over 900 passengers but mostly for a select, much-reduced 600 on the ship's long, luxurious, expensive cruises. Painted in distinctive green, she was commissioned – a symbol of British rebirth in shipbuilding – in December 1948. Another British shipowner, Union-Castle Line, was not far behind. They built their biggest liners yet, the 28,700-ton *Pretoria Castle* and *Edinburgh Castle*, for the UK–South Africa run. Meanwhile, London-based P&O and the Orient Line embarked on a vast rebuilding programme, beginning in 1948, that included no less than seven big liners. Elsewhere, and for their colonial services, the Dutch added the 23,100grt *Willem Ruys* while the French finished their 17,300-ton *La Marseillaise*. Portugal added four new liners for trading to colonial Africa while the Belgians commissioned no less than five ships for its operations to and from the Congo. For the trans-Pacific run, American President Lines added a pair of splendid twin-stackers, the *President Cleveland* and *President Wilson* in 1947–48. Combo ships – that blended 100–200 passengers with considerable cargo capacities – were extremely popular from the late 1940s onwards.

In the 1950s the whole industry boomed – more and more passengers were travelling by ship. From Atlantic liners to those headed to South America to migrant ships to Melbourne and Sydney, every berth, it seemed, was booked. Each year of the decade produced new liners. America invested in several, including the brilliant *United States*, Italy rebuilt its fleet, the Dutch and Scandinavians added fresh tonnage and then there were some innovative ships such as the engines-aft design of the *Southern Cross* and 'no smokestacks' for the *Rotterdam*. New companies rose in the ranks as well, such as Italy's Costa Line.

We have a created a diverse list of passenger ships – some large and very famous, others smaller and all but lost to the back drawers of maritime history. But each ship tells something of the history of 1950s ocean liner travel. The ships themselves are like actresses: they have lives, stories and sometimes play many roles. The 1958-built *Brasil*, included in these pages, had eight different names in her forty-five years. Of course, very few of these ships endure to this day, with the obvious exception of the long-idle *United States* and the moored hotel-museum *Rotterdam*.

But, in deep nostalgia, I think back to, say, a summer's day near my home, in New York Harbor, in the 1950s and when members of this cast – the *Independence*, *United States*, *Andrea Doria, Maasdam, Kungsholm* and *Olympia* – might be in port at the same time. What a collection of passenger ships! Here are some of the *Great Passenger Ships 1950–1960*.

Bill Miller
Secaucus, New Jersey
2016

1

YANKEE TWINS: *INDEPENDENCE & CONSTITUTION (1951)*

They were the biggest American liners to be built after the Second World War. They were also the first new liners for New York–Mediterranean service in almost twenty years, since 1932. And, as the ultimate maritime symbols of post-war Yankee genius and innovation, they were the first fully air-conditioned large liners to put to sea. Expectedly, they attracted great attention when they came into service in the enthusiastic, high pitch of the early 1950s. Built by Bethlehem Steel Company's Quincy, Massachusetts,

yard, they were commissioned as the *Independence* and *Constitution*. Their owners, New York City-based American Export Lines, were besieged with requests for information about them and received bookings as far as a year ahead. The 29,500-ton *Independence* had her debut in February 1951; her sister followed in June the next year. They were strong and well built – with the *Independence* lasting some fifty-seven years.

Originally, the 23-knot sisters were scheduled on three-week round voyages: New York to Algeciras, Cannes, Genoa and Naples. They carried exactly 1,000 passengers – 295 in first class, 375 cabin class and 330 tourist class. Minimum fares to Italy in their maiden year were $335 in first class, $260 cabin class and $205 in tourist.

'They were great ships with top first-class accommodations,' added Herb Maletz, who was assistant comptroller in American Export's Lower Broadway headquarters:

> They had fantastic wine cellars, for example, that were selected by Alexis Lecchine himself. There was French silver service and live music at dinner in first class. You could have a steak at three in the morning if you wanted. Everything was done with great style. The first ten to twelve years were very successful financially. Things did not fade for these two liners until the mid '60s.

In the 1950s, in those last years before airline dominance, the 683ft-long *Independence* and *Constitution* sailed in direct competition with the new luxury ships of the Italian Line, namely the *Andrea Doria* and *Cristoforo*

American design: the *Constitution* sails off from its builders yard at Quincy, Massachusetts, in the spring of 1951. (ALF collection)

Replenishment: the 683ft-long *Constitution* rests between Mediterranean voyages on the north side of Pier 84, at the foot of West 44th Street in Manhattan. (ALF collection)

First class on board the *Independence* and *Constitution* often included celebrities, both from the entertainment and the political worlds. Peter Ustinov, Cary Grant, Gina Lollobrigida and Katherine Hepburn were among those listed on manifests. 'Grace Kelly was, of course, the most publicised when she sailed with us for her wedding in Monaco in April 1956,' recalled Maletz:

We allowed Miss Kelly to keep her dog in her stateroom, U-101, on board the *Constitution*. But there was quite a mess afterward. We also had 100–200 wedding guests in blocks of rooms and at least 100 reporters and photographers. The ship was specially detoured to Monaco and then anchored in Monte Carlo harbor. Miss Kelly left by barge, but gusts of wind blew at her hat and skirt, and all in front of squads of photographers! On several occasions, we had Ibn Saud, the Saudi Arabian king. The ships were diverted several times to meet or drop him off at Casablanca. He was an extraordinary passenger. He gave $1,000 tips as well as gold Rolex watches to the staff. Even a simple bow from a steward warranted a tip, perhaps a $100 bill. A treasurer with a small suitcase followed the king everywhere on board …

We also had lots of high-ranking military officers and their families in first class. The enlisted men were in cabin class. In tourist class, we also had lots of Italian immigrants going westbound. And there were huge numbers of Catholic

Colombo. 'We were equal, if not better, in some ways to the Italian Line at that time,' added Maletz:

When they were first conceived, in 1948–49, John Slater, the financial genius who was then president of American Export, wanted big liners like the United States Lines. But he insisted that these three-class ships must also be like cruise ships, like our 125-passenger, all-first-class 'Four Aces' [*Excalibur, Excambion, Exeter* and *Exochorda*]. He believed that there would be passengers [aboard the *Independence* and *Constitution*] making the roundtrip, a three-week cruise, New York to the Mediterranean and back again. And so, a man – brought over from San Francisco's Matson Line – invented 'Sunlane Cruises'. These were voyages of 21–23 days and where the added ports varied. We'd call variously at Casablanca, Malaga, Funchal and Las Palmas. We were always testing.

Great size: in her maiden year, in October 1951, the mighty 29,500grt *Constitution* takes a turn in dry dock at Bethlehem Steel's Key Highway shipyard in Baltimore. The sight of the big liner in dry dock drew crowds. (James McNamara collection)

Sister ships: the *Independence* and *Constitution* pass one another in the Narrows, in New York's Lower Bay. (ALF collection)

priests and nuns coming and going. American Export always had good contacts with the Roman Catholic Church on both sides of the Atlantic.

The two sisters were extensively refitted in the winter of 1959 and had their capacities increased by 110 berths. But that March, on the return from the Newport News shipyard in Virginia, the 683ft-long *Constitution* made front-page headlines. She rammed and cut in two the 15,000-ton Norwegian tanker *Jalanta* outside the entrance to New York Harbor. 'The master was going too fast and cut corners because he had an early appointment in Manhattan. It seems he did not want to be late for the dentist,' reported Herb Maletz:

The *Constitution* had damages and so had to go directly to Bethlehem Steel's 56th yard in Brooklyn. The repairs were extensive and the ship missed several sailings. The two sections of the *Jalanta* were brought to Bethlehem's Hoboken plant and were later welded together and repaired. It all cost American Export millions. Expectedly, the captain of the *Constitution* was fired.

The two liners were repainted with all-white hulls in 1960 and were also joined by the smaller *Atlantic*, a converted freighter. But by the mid 1960s,

MAY 1
MAY 13
MAY 24

THREE TO GO!

Enjoy one of these 3 wonderful Sunlane Cruises to the Mediterranean

Make this a May you'll always remember Choose any one of these 3 cruises . and see the Mediterranean in its May-time beauty

MAY 1 – S.S. INDEPENDENCE – 21 delightful days, visiting Casablanca, Gibraltar Palermo, Naples, Genoa, Cannes and Madeira. Returning to New York May 22.

MAY 13 – S.S. CONSTITUTION – 19 days along the Sunlane route, visiting Casablanca, Naples, Genoa and Cannes. Returning to New York June 1.

MAY 24 – S.S. INDEPENDENCE – 22 sunlit days, visiting Casablanca, Gibraltar Palermo, Naples, Genoa, Cannes and Madeira. Returning June 15.

Cabin Class cruise fares begin at $603, and First Class at $767 – a lavish value for your travel dollar. See your travel agent today for more information. And remember, if you can't get away in May there are also attractive Sunlane cruises August through December.

S.S. CONSTITUTION   S.S. INDEPENDENCE

AMERICAN EXPORT LINES

Bon voyage: the handsome-looking *Independence* outbound at New York in a view dated 1959. (ALF collection)

Sunlane Cruises: advertising for the American Export sister ships in 1957. (National Geographic Society)

the *Independence* and *Constitution* had huge losses. The Mediterranean trade was declining. American seagoing labour was expensive, there were disruptive strikes and American Export itself was late in re-adapting to the more lucrative cruise trades. The Fugazy Travel Company became more involved and then convinced American Export to refit and restyle the *Independence* at a Baltimore shipyard as a 'go-go cruise ship', which included $1 million Japanese-style sunburst exterior paint job. In the modern era of art deco cruises, they ran discount cruises – seven days from New York to San Juan and St Thomas for $98 sans food! It all failed miserably.

Running deeper and deeper into the red and with little hope in sight, American Export lost interest and the two liners were laid up – the *Independence* at Baltimore in March 1969 and the *Constitution* at Jacksonville, Florida, five months later. Expectedly, rumours circulated. Italy's Flotta Lauro was said to be interested in them as were the Greek owners of the laid-up *Caribia*, Cunard's former *Caronia*. In 1970, it was reported that Chandris Lines would buy both the *Constitution* and American President Lines' *President Roosevelt*, but in fact took only the latter. Instead, the two Export liners sat – sad, lonely, rusting. They were finally cleared by the US Government, in March 1974, to be sold to one of C.Y. Tung's affiliate companies, the Atlantic Far East Line. Renamed *Oceanic Independence* and *Oceanic Constitution*, they

sailed with skeleton crews for Hong Kong, but not much else. While there were plans for further service – Pacific cruising initially – the dramatic rise in marine fuel oil prices, from $35 to $95 per ton, shelved all plans, at least temporarily. They would not resume commercial sailing for several more years, until 1980 and 1982, and then for a brand-new company, American Hawaii Cruises.

Luxury Liner Row: grand gathering on a summer's day, in a view dated 1965, with (from back to front) *Sylvania, Queen Mary, Leonardo da Vinci, France, Bremen, United States, Hanseatic* and *Constitution.* (ALF collection)

The *Independence*, reconfigured for 900 one-class passengers, remained in Hawaiian service for twenty-one years. She had a major, life-extending refit in 1994, sailing to and from the Newport News shipyard in Virginia via the Panama Canal. 'Greater maintenance and higher operating costs were of course part of operating the ageing "Indy" as we called her,' noted American Hawaii vice president Bill Anunsen in 2001:

We had lots of spare parts for the *Independence* taken from her sister, the *Constitution,* which sank off Hawaii in November 1997 while empty and being towed from Portland, Oregon to an Asian scrap yard. The *Constitution* had not been refitted in the '90s like the *Independence* and was laid up at Portland in early 1996. Of course, very few of the original, 1950–51 manufacturers of parts for the *Independence* remained in business fifty years later. But even the few that remain, these do not make parts from the 1950s. Existing parts, both those in

use and those held as spares in warehouses in Honolulu harbor, have long lives, however. Bethlehem Steel, the builder, used the very finest equipment and mechanical parts.

'We run the *Independence* at only 12–14 knots in Hawaiian islands cruising,' added Anunsen:

Her seven-day itinerary out of Maui is balanced between morning and evening departures. Channel crossings were made at night when the passengers were usually asleep. There are no stabilisers on the *Independence*, but she always rode very well. She is a very solid ship, built to very high US Government standards. Any rough spots in sailing came late night and therefore caused the least inconvenience. She burned 2,700–2,800 barrels of fuel oil, which costs 30 per cent more in Hawaii than in US mainland ports. The newer, 1983-built *Patriot* (ex-*Nieuw Amsterdam*), as a comparison, burns 1,800 barrels.

In Hawaiian service, the *Independence* had a crew of 330, all of whom were either US citizens or registered aliens:

She had one of the youngest hotel staffs at sea and one of the friendliest, most smiling crews anywhere. There were 12–18 week rotations with 6-week leaves. She was a great training ground for crewmembers as well as a good place for upgrading licenses and certificates. The youngish crew had a great passion and their goal was to make memories. In the end, the *Independence* reached her third generation of making memories in the Pacific. She was actually a moving piece of Hawaii. From stem to stern, the *Independence* was Hawaiiana!

After the dramatic and drastic downturns in worldwide travel following the terrorist attacks of 11 September 2001, American Hawaii Cruises lost a huge number of passengers and then quickly slipped into bankruptcy. Finally, the *Independence* sailed empty to San Francisco and, by December 2001, was moored at Alameda, quiet and lifeless and being prepared to take a place in the US Government's 'mothball fleet' of ships in reserve at nearby Suisun Bay.

Soon and almost expectedly, a few flash rumours surfaced: using the ship in future as a museum ship or a military rest and recreation centre for battle crews out in the Middle East or as a combination moored hotel and casino.

In September 2006, in the aftermath of Hurricane Katrina, it was reported that she would be moved to New Orleans for use as temporary housing. Meanwhile, Miami-based Norwegian Cruise Lines had renewed interest in establishing a US-flag cruise division and their plans included restoration not only of the long-idle *United States*, but the *Independence* as well. Enthusiasts seemed excited, but nothing came to pass. Instead, the faded *Independence* (later renamed *Oceanic* and then *Platinum II*) – minus her main mast, which had been removed for bridge clearance – remained idle at the former Bethlehem Steel shipyard in San Francisco.

In 2008, the former *Independence* was towed to India, to be deliberately run aground at Alang in India for scrapping. But she unintentionally ran aground in the outer bay, later broke in two and finally had to be demolished on the spot.

Winter's night: the *Independence* and *Constitution* rest during their annual overhauls at the Bethlehem Steel shipyard in Hoboken in a photo dated January 1964. (Bethlehem Steel Corporation)

High above Pier 84 in 1965 with the *Atlantic* on the left and the *Constitution* on the right. (ALF collection)

The *Independence* and her sister remain interesting and very appealing. 'By 2010, these ships are absolutely beloved and always quick sellers for collectors and this includes their later American Hawaii days,' noted ocean liner collector and dealer Brian Hawley. 'But good items from the *Independence* and *Constitution* under American Export are actually quite hard to find. Recently, I found a very rare isometric deck plan for these sisters and it was an instant seller.'

2

ECONOMY TWINS: *RYNDAM & MAASDAM (1951–52)*

In the late 1940s, the transatlantic liner trade bubbled into a post-war boom. The directors of the illustrious Holland America Line had a vision, a clear look at the future of ocean travel, centred on economy travel, the inexpensive but very profitable trade in tourist class. More and more passengers, they felt, would want inexpensive but comfortable accommodation. First class would be offered but reduced; in fact, it would be retained only to conform to Atlantic passenger ship conference standards. Furthermore, there would be no second or cabin class. New tourist tonnage would not have to be either large or fast, but moderate. They would be practical passenger ships. The company had been planning, as part of its post-war rebuilding programme, two sixty-passenger combination passenger-cargo ships for its North Europe–Caribbean–Panama Canal–North American west coast trade. These 11,000-tonners were to be named *Dinteldyk* and *Diemerdyk*. The keel plates for the first of them were laid in place in December 1949, at the

Wilton-Fijenoord shipyard at Schiedam. Then, quite suddenly, company thinking changed – the priority would be toward full passenger ships with far larger capacities and aimed at the North Atlantic tourist trade.

The design for the *Dinteldyk* was completely reworked. The ship would become the 15,000-ton *Ryndam* (a name derived from the River Rhine). Replacing the initial six cargo holds would be seven passenger decks. The thirty-nine berths in first class were contained entirely on the upper boat deck, in what was described as the penthouse section of the 503ft-long ship. There was a small, separate dining room, combined lounge and smoking room, and partially enclosed promenade. All the first-class cabins had private bathrooms.

The tourist-class spaces occupied the major portion of the *Ryndam*. Overall, tourist class occupied 90 per cent of the ship, utilising five decks. In tourist class, with 836 berths, 63 per cent of the cabins were doubles. There were also six singles, twenty-eight triples and fifty-six four-berth cabins. Very few of these cabins had private facilities. Instead, passengers used public lavatories, showers and tub baths conveniently located on each deck.

The concept of tourist-class dominance was a great success and soon spread. It was subsequently copied by the likes of Cunard for its *Saxonia*, *Ivernia*, *Carinthia* and *Sylvania* (1954–57), and by Canadian Pacific for their *Empress of Britain* and *Empress of England* (1956–57).

The single-screw, 16-knot *Ryndam* was launched on 16 December 1950. Her intended sister ship, the projected *Diemerdyk*, had also been redesigned and became their *Maasdam*. The *Ryndam* first crossed from Rotterdam, via Le Havre, Southampton and Cobh, to New York in July 1951; the *Maasdam* followed in August 1952. The pair were immediately acclaimed as outstanding, novel ships, where passengers could enjoy comforts in tourist class for as little as $20 per person per day or $160 for the eight-day passage between New York and Southampton. The *Ryndam* and *Maasdam* quickly became known as 'the economy twins'. They were highly successful, had

Main headquarters: the 503ft-long *Maasdam* berthed at the Wilhelminakade, Rotterdam, the corporate seat of the Holland America Line. (ALF collection)

PERFECT SUMMER VACATIONS WITH PLAY!

in the breeze-cooled West Indies

(leaving July 22 and August 22)

NEW VACATION IDEA · 14 DAYS · FROM $295
SAIL FROM HISTORIC MONTREAL AND QUEBEC
aboard the popular, fully air-conditioned, stabilizer-equipped regular transatlantic liner **RYNDAM** July 22, for 14 fun*tastic* days. Party all the way, *and* frolic in Nassau and Miami! Rates—from only $295. Better hurry . . . last year this cruise sold out fast!

. . . OR SAIL FROM EXCITING NEW YORK aboard the transatlantic liner **MAASDAM** (fully air-conditioned—and stabilizer-equipped) **August 22**, for 14 equally fun-packed days. (And just think! No Labor Day traffic!) Explore Nassau, Curacao, Kingston and Port-au-Prince. Rates—from $350.

See your travel agent for details on both cruises. (Better do it soon. Our uniquely festive cruises are invariably *the* favorites of America's cruise vacationers.)

"It's good to be on a well-run ship"

Holland-America Line
29 Broadway, New York 6 · WHitehall 4-1900

Cruising: 1957 advertising for the sisters *Maasdam* and *Ryndam*. (Author's collection)

Busy day: (from left to right) the *Statendam*, *Noordam* and *Maasdam* at Hoboken in September 1957. (Port Authority of New York & New Jersey)

90 per cent occupancy and paid for themselves very quickly. In almost quick time, they prompted Holland America to plan for a larger, more luxurious version, the 24,000-ton *Statendam* of 1957.

The *Ryndam* and *Maasdam* had two further distinctions. They were the first Holland America liners to have dove-grey hulls and a most unusual funnel design. Originally intended to have black hulls, the lighter grey colouring was selected for superior heat-deflecting qualities, especially in winter when the two ships would be sent on Caribbean cruises. The light grey also assisted the full air-conditioning systems. The funnels, the result of considerable testing, were selected because of their smoke- and soot-deflecting abilities. Provisional sketches had shown rather conventional, almost paint-can stacks, but different designs, created by the French Air Force, were selected for the two liners. Wafer thin and tapered on top, they were named Strombous Aerofoil. They directed smoke away from the ship, but were only quite successful in some ways. The design was not used, however, aboard any future Holland America ships.

Neither vessel was ever a good 'sea boat' (they pitched tremendously at sea). The late Everett Viez, a travel agent and ocean liner historian, once remarked, 'Seasickness was common on the *Ryndam* and *Maasdam*. Some passengers and staff even joked that seasickness was part of the daily activity sheet.' They were later fitted with fin stabilisers, which helped 'to some extent'.

After the new *Rotterdam* entered service in September 1959, the *Ryndam* was, after over eight years, released from the New York run. Beginning in April 1960, she opened a new Holland America service – from Rotterdam, Le Havre and Southampton to Québec City and Montreal. Soon afterwards, the *Ryndam* also had a new, off-season role – she was used as a 'floating university'. Chartered to an American college, she became known as the 'World Campus Afloat' and began two around-the-world voyages, one in autumn and the other in winter, with teachers, guest lecturers and about 500 students on board. Subjects and courses were linked to the ports of call. This cruise concept continues to date, most recently using the luxurious former German liner *Deutschland*.

The *Ryndam* was transferred in September 1966 to a Holland America subsidiary, the Europe-Canada Line, which used West German registry, officers and crew. Thirteen months later, however, the ship returned to Dutch registry, but was assigned to another arm of Holland America: the Hague-based Trans-Ocean Steamship Company. That company had operated three converted

Sailing day: the rebuilt *Stefan Batory*, the former *Maasdam*, departs from Gdynia. (Polish Ocean Lines)

Victory-class freighters, renamed *Groote Beer*, *Waterman* and *Zuiderkruis*, which were used in low-fare tourist, student and migrant services. In April 1968, the *Ryndam* was renamed *Waterman*, but then reverted to *Ryndam* within six months. Meanwhile, the *Maasdam* had replaced her sister ship on the seasonal Canadian trade and then, in another new venture, began off-season winter service from Rotterdam and Southampton to Australia via Suez.

But time was running out – the liner trades had changed and quite drastically by the late 1960s. In October 1968, the *Maasdam* was sold off to the Polish Ocean Lines, refitted as the *Stefan Batory* and used on the North Atlantic, between Gdynia, Copenhagen, London, Québec City and Montreal, beginning in April 1969. She replaced the veteran, 33-year-old *Batory*. Used also for winter cruising, the *Stefan Batory* traded for almost twenty years before the Greek-owned Lelakis Group, parent of Regency Cruises, bought the idle 15,000-ton ship, which was renamed *Stefan* in 1988. These new owners planned to refit her for further cruising, but the project never materialised. She sat idle for some twelve years – rusting, dark, largely unattended. In March 2000, however, she made one final short voyage: over to the scrappers in Aliaga in Turkey. The ex-*Maasdam* was by then 48 years old.

After being decommissioned in 1971, the *Ryndam* sat idle for a year before, in summer 1972, being sold for $2½ million to Greece's Epirotiki Lines. She was thoroughly modernised, given a restyled, sleek funnel and refitted with modern public rooms as well as a lido deck with pool. All her cabins, for a total of 731 all-first-class passengers, now had private bathrooms.

Renamed *Atlas*, she seemed a 'new ship' in many ways. She entered service in May 1973 as Epirotiki's competition to rival Sun Line's *Stella Solaris*, the converted former French combo ship *Cambodge*. Used initially on seven-day Aegean/Eastern Mediterranean cruises from Piraeus, the *Atlas* later cruised to Norway, the Baltic, the Caribbean and on cruises from Rio de Janeiro to lower South America. 'Once in Greek service, the *Atlas*,' as remembered by the late ship designer Arthur Crook, 'was always short of electric power and so Andreas Potomianos [owner-partner of Epirotiki Lines] used to buy second-hand generators and place them all over the ship. In the end, there were twelve of them on board.'

'The exterior of the *Atlas* was created by a young designer named John Bannerman,' added Crook:

> Epirotiki wanted something new and different – and sleek that would match or surpass the new Karageorgis ferries, the sleek *Mediterranean Sea* and *Mediterranean Sky*. Karageorgis was threatening to Epirotiki then – and Greek shipowners were extremely competitive. There was also the appearance of the greatly rebuilt *Stella Solaris* for another rival company, the Sun Line. They were, of course, all older, rebuilt ships, but they had to look new, modern, stylish.

In 1980, however, the *Atlas* was reportedly to be sold to Mexican interests, who planned to use her as the condominium-style cruise ship *Royal Prince*. This never materialised.

The great slowdown in Mediterranean crusing in 1985–86 following the hijacking of the *Achille Lauro* and events in the Middle East actually finished off the *Atlas*. She was often laid up, cancelled some sailings and made at least one cruise with as few as fifty passengers aboard. Other ships and their owners were suffering as well. The *Atlas* was soon sold off, becoming the casino ship *Pride of Mississippi* and later the *Pride of Galveston* for short gambling jaunts in the Gulf of Mexico out of US ports. This phase lasted for about five years.

Mechanically worn out by 1993, she was sold yet again, this time to Nevada gambling interests who used her as the permanently moored *Copa Casino* at Gulfport, Mississippi. Finally, in 2003, she was again offered for sale, but this time going to the scrappers. It was an unfortunate end. While under tow, in March 2004, the 52-year-old former *Ryndam* sank in the eastern Caribbean, while en route to Indian breakers at far-off Alang.

3

NEW ITALIANS FOR AUSTRALIA (1951)

In the early 1950s, to replace their severe losses during the Second World War, Trieste-based Lloyd Triestino built three sets of very handsome sister ships and near-sister ships. All of them were in the large passenger-cargo class. Three were for Europe–Australia service, two for Africa and a final pair for the Far Eastern run. Each of them was especially sleek with domed funnels, raked masts above their wheelhouses and well-balanced, all-white hulls.

The first trio – the *Australia*, *Neptunia* and *Oceania* – were constructed in 1951 by Cantieri Riuniti dell'Adriatico at Trieste. At 13,100grt, they carried passengers in three classes – 280 in first class, 120 second class and 392 in third class. They sailed monthly, at monthly intervals, from Genoa, Naples and Messina for Port Said, Suez, Aden, Colombo, Djakarta, Fremantle, Melbourne and Sydney, and then the same ports in reverse. Later, in 1956, when the Suez Canal was closed, they sailed via South Africa.

Each of these ships was decorated in contemporary, post-war Italian styling, had air conditioning and their amenities included two outdoor pools (one for first and another for second class). British passenger ship connoisseur C.M. Squarey visited the *Neptunia* in her maiden season, in October 1951. Among other comments, in his book *The Patient Talks*, he wrote:

When looking over this ship, I had with me a colonel serving with the British forces at Trieste, a man of some discernment and not the type that is voluble to praise over anything. It was interesting to hear his impartial impression of this new ship. He gave the *Neptunia* high marks for everything. I do, also, the more since her size does not put her, in football parlance, in the same 'division' as some other post-war ships in the Australia trade. In their booklet describing the ship, I don't think the owners have done her full justice because the drawings make the rooms look severe and harsh, and the coloring is too vivid. Otherwise,

The three-class *Oceania* arriving at Melbourne. (ALF collection)

I sum her up as a proud-looking ship that within has made the most of every ton of her tonnage. The *Neptunia* and her two sisters should form a very good trio, capable of showing the Italian flag in a fine way in a young country where the emigrants of today may well turn out to be the industrial magnates of tomorrow. Good sowing now may reap a good harvest in years to come. And these ships must be sowing good seed.

The three ships were refitted and upgraded in 1958. Changes on the Italy–Australia trade included the elimination of second class as well as the old third class. And so, berthing on the *Australia* was restyled as 136 in first class and 536 in tourist class. But further changes lay ahead. In 1960, the *Neptunia* was experimentally changed to an all-one-class ship. But soon after, Italian Government-owned Lloyd Triestino looked not only to bigger, but better, brand-new tonnage for the Australian trade, namely the 27,000-ton 1,700-passenger *Guglielmo Marconi* and *Galileo Galilei* of 1963. Competition on the busy Australian run was developing at an almost furious, if final, pace. P&O-Orient had just added the biggest Australia-routed liners of all, the 41,000-ton *Oriana* and then the 45,000-ton *Canberra*. Another British

shipowner, the Shaw Savill Line, took on the *Northern Star*. Greece's Chandris Lines was expanding with the 1,600-passenger *Ellinis* and, amongst the Italians themselves, Cogedar Line had just added the *Flavia*, Sitmar planned for the 1,900-berth *Fairstar* and Flotta Lauro talked of two brand-new 27,000-tonners.

The three older ships were transferred, with the Finmare Group, to the Italian Line in 1963. Respectively, they were renamed *Donizetti*, *Rossini* and *Verdi*. Dubbed the 'Three Musicians', they worked the Italy–West Coast of South America route (Genoa, Naples, Cannes, Barcelona and Tenerife across to La Guaira, Curaçao, Cartagena, Cristobal and the Panama Canal, Buenaventura, Puna, Callao, Arica, Antofagasta and finally Valparaiso). They sailed for thirteen years until, with vast cutbacks in the Finmare passenger fleet, they were withdrawn and laid up in 1976. While they might have been rebuilt as cruise ships, they could not find new owners and so were scrapped (at La Spezia, near Genoa) a year later. In his superb *From Emigrant Ships to Luxury Liners*, author Peter Plowman made a keen observation about this trio: 'These three liners all came from the same shipyard and within months of one another, spent their entire careers operating together and then ended their lives at the same place within months of each other.'

Restyled for Italy–South America service, the *Donizetti* was one of Italian Line's so-called 'Three Musicians'. (Alex Duncan)

4

SPEED QUEEN: SS *UNITED STATES* (1952)

Even though there were no celebrations, at least in New York, on 3 July 2002, it was a rather special date in maritime history, especially in American maritime history. Exactly fifty years earlier, the super liner *United States* left her berth at Pier 86, at the foot of West 46th Street, and began her remarkable maiden voyage. She made the crossing from New York to England in three days, ten hours and forty minutes, and captured the prized Blue Riband of the Atlantic. (Earlier, she had done up to 43 knots on her trials off the Virginia Capes and also did as much as 20 knots in reverse. One of her engineers later told the author that the liner was absolutely capable of as much as 50 knots.) A true military secret in that age of Cold War relations, the 990ft-long ship had over 241,000hp compared to 158,000hp on board her nearest rival, the *Queen Mary*. Triumphantly, the 53,300-ton Yankee flagship brought great honour to her nation, to her owners and to those who designed and built her. Instantly, the *United States* became the most famous, most publicised and most popular ship afloat. 'There was nothing quite like her in the 1950s,' remembered a British friend, himself a one-time captain of merchant ships. 'She was the floating pride of America. She symbolised the brilliant technology of what was then the most advanced country on earth – and perhaps the ultimate victor of the Second World War.'

Although she sailed commercially for only seventeen years, she is well remembered to this date. I am continually asked about her status. Will she sail again? Can she be converted to a contemporary cruise ship? Or will she be used as a stationary museum or floating hotel? On the ocean liner collectibles market, she is of top interest and one of the highest priced, ranking with the likes of the ill-fated *Titanic* and the ultra-extravagant *Normandie*. A cocktail glass, a silver serving tray or a long-faded stateroom footstool fetch hefty prices. Even an out-of-print biography sold recently for as much as $300.

The *United States* was innovation, a great success, a grand flag-waver. The late maritime author and historian Frank Braynard once dubbed her a 'star spangled giant'. The $75 million ship was, of course, created totally for a different era with different needs and different concerns. She grew out of the Second World War, when Washington saw big liners as useful troopships should another military emergency develop. To many, in the late 1940s, a Third World War was not unthinkable. Within days, the 1,725-passenger, three-class *United States* could be converted to transport more than 15,000 soldier-passengers. The Pentagon was much enthused – and helped design the ship. She had military ingredients: extra thick hull plating, no wood, a back-up engine room, a large fuel capacity and even fire-retardant bedspreads and drapes in the staterooms.

But America and the ship's owners, the United States Lines, also wanted a serious contender and player on the still-lucrative commercial transatlantic passenger run to and from Europe. Such a new liner had to be a serious rival to the Europeans, namely the British, with their celebrated pair *Queen Mary* and *Queen Elizabeth*. 'American ships had been in the shadows, in second place, on the North Atlantic for far too long,' added Frank Braynard, who was aboard the ship's delivery voyage in June 1952.

To many, she was a very special ship. 'She was the Blue Riband holder and the very fastest liner anywhere,' said the late Michael Shernoff, a staff member in the 1960s. 'She was not an especially elegant liner, but was immaculate, impeccably maintained and provided the highest level of American service and cuisine at sea.' Peter Knego, a maritime author, photographer and collector of ocean liner fittings added, 'The *United States* and the two *Queens* were my first exposure to ocean liners apart from the *Titanic*. The *United States* was featured in the *World Book Encyclopedia* and, once envisioned, she never left my thoughts. Those big, streamlined funnels and her sleek, low profile were especially modern to my mid-Sixties eyes.'

Many were impressed by the liner's appearance, even calling her one of the most beautiful and striking passenger ships of all time. 'Her hull and

Just after being named and floating, the great *United States* is moved to a fitting-out berth at the Newport News shipyard. (United States Lines)

Dressed in flags: off and away on her record-breaking maiden voyage, on 3 July 1952. (ALF collection)

superstructure were, in a word, great,' reported designer and ocean liner collector Mario Pulice:

> The balance of her long, sleek hull, knife-edged bow, low superstructure and all capped by those incredible and massive tear-shaped funnels was truly a sight. Unfortunately, I never saw her in her heyday, but have seen her many times in lay-up, at Norfolk and later Philadelphia. Whenever I 'visited' her even in the shabby state of lay-up, I was always struck by her stature. She is a very proud ship in the water. She even looks like she's a very fast ship even when tied-up! I am always impressed by the balance of her exterior, something that all ships do not have, especially those being built today.

She also stimulated patriotic feelings. Michael Shernoff noted:

> While I was only a seasonal crewmember on her, I felt enormously proud of her and how she represented the USA on the Atlantic. She was a mighty symbol of American ingenuity, style and technology. Seeing those great red, white and blue funnels lit up at night at Bremerhaven, Le Havre or Southampton always

During a seamen's strike, America's four largest and most luxurious liners rest quietly at Piers 84 and 86 – the *United States* (top), *America, Independence* and *Constitution*. (United States Lines)

Five days to Southampton or Le Havre aboard the speedy *United States*. (Author's collection)

Pier 86, New York, the terminal for the *United States*. (United States Lines)

Grand gathering, Luxury Liner Row in 1952: (from left to right) *Independence, United States, Liberté, Queen Elizabeth, Caronia* and *Franconia*. (Photofest)

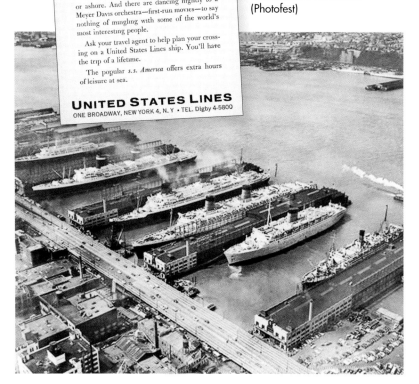

elicited a surge of patriotic pride in so far as this was a symbol of America's peacetime might and power.

In the 1950s, the *United States* superbly filled her commercial role, sailing between New York, Southampton, Le Havre and Bremerhaven for some eleven months of each year. She averaged well over 90 per cent capacity per season. Fortunately, she was never called to war duty. Even during the tense Cuban Missile Crisis of October 1962, the Pentagon put the more moderately

The 990ft-long *United States* arriving at the Ocean Terminal, Southampton. (ALF collection)

sized liners *Argentina* and *Brasil* on standby alert rather than the mighty and mightily expensive *United States*. But in the 1960s it was all changing. The jet gave the airlines an even greater hold on transoceanic travel and so big liners like the labour- and fuel-costly *United States* became less and less viable. They lost clientele, of course, as well. The ship lost money and then even more money. By 1968–69, she was running deeply in the red. Furthermore, the government had lost interest in her. There would be, they predicted, little if any need for a big troopship in the future.

In November 1969, the wondrous *United States* began her long sleep: lay-up, darkness, stripping down, decay, then deepening decay, and all with a continually uncertain future.

It might be interesting to note that the four greatest liners produced in US shipyards after the Second World War never reached the scrappers. While the rust-streaked, badly faded *United States* languishes at her Philadelphia berth, her one-time running mate, the smaller *America*, broke in half on the north end of the Canary Islands while under tow and then ran aground in January 1994. First, the aft section drifted into the sea and sank; later, in April 2007, the 400ft-long forward section, which seemed 'locked' on the rocky coast, also collapsed into the sea. At the time of the grounding, then renamed *American Star*, she was being towed around Africa from Greece to Thailand for further use as a floating hotel at Bangkok. Of the other two liners, the *Constitution* sank in the Pacific, in November 1997, while empty and being

During her maiden crossing in July 1952, with paint peeled off the forward bow section. (Alex Duncan)

towed to a Far Eastern scrap yard. Lastly, the long-idle former *Independence* was towed to India in 2008, but grounded before being beached at Alang, broke in half and then had to be demolished where she laid.

By November 2015, the *United States* had been silent and idle for forty-six years – indeed, longer than any liner in history. In those years, there had been countless stories, rumours and hints of revival – or at least a final ending. That November, she had been given further funding to remain at her Philadelphia berth, but, while yet another study was under way, this one possibly to convert the ship to diesel propulsion. Also, the idea of a moored gambling and entertainment centre was again on the table, as was her use as a floating power plant moored at Brooklyn – in fact, adjacent to the passenger ship terminal in Red Hook, which is used by the *Queen Mary 2*. Then there was preliminary planning about scrapping the *United States*, at nearby Chester, Pennsylvania, or in Bordentown, New Jersey, or, after an expensive tow, at Brownsville, Texas. Indeed, there is more to be written yet in the history of the SS *United States*.

5

ANDREA DORIA AND THE NEW ITALIANS (1952)

When I met with Maurizio Eliseo, at the giant Chantiers de l'Atlantique shipyard at Saint-Nazaire in western France, where he was employed as a project supervisor in the building of the 150,000-ton *Queen Mary 2*, the largest liner yet created, it had been little more than fifty years since the *Andrea Doria* steamed into New York Harbor for the first time. Despite the chilly, rain-filled atmosphere of that January morning in 1953, the tone for the Italian Line was jubilant. There were fluttering flags, tooting horns and screeching sirens, and of course an escorting armada of tugs, fireboats and ferries. Slowly, she made her way up along the Hudson and then to her berth at Pier 84, Italian Line's terminal at the foot of West 44th Street. Yes, she was a very beautiful-looking ship, modern and sleek, and on the inside she was a tour de force of contemporary design. But more importantly, her completion

The 700ft-long *Andrea Doria* was the post-war pride of the Italian merchant marine. (ALF collection)

Clean and tidy: even on cold winter days, crew members tend to the exterior of the beautiful *Andrea Doria*. (ALF collection)

signalled the triumphant return of the Italians to the prestigious, demanding, highly competitive and always nationalistic transatlantic run. Out of the ashes of the Second World War, the Italian merchant marine was rebuilding. The *Doria*'s first appearance was called, by at least one newspaper (*New York Times*), 'the rebirth, the renaissance, of Italy's fleet'.

In the late 1940s, when Italy had lost just about all of her passenger ships, the Italian Line desperately needed to revive its passenger services and also build replacement tonnage. The four largest post-war survivors, the liners *Saturnia*, *Vulcania*, *Conte Biancamano* and *Conte Grande*, had been seized and were still in American hands. Reports suggested that the *Saturnia* and *Vulcania*, no longer needed for Allied military duties, were to be sold off to the Soviets. President Alcide de Gaspari decided to travel to Washington, to plead with President Harry Truman and also with members of the senate. He won in the end and promised, in appreciation, to send the 'most beautiful new ships' to America. He even succeeded in having the Allied post-war ban

Three liners at Genoa: the *Cristoforo Colombo*, the French *Bretagne* and the *Augustus*. (Richard Faber collection)

Eclectic decor: the unique Zodiac Suite aboard the 1,248-passenger *Andrea Doria*. (ALF collection)

Twins: the *Andrea Doria* and her sister ship, the *Cristoforo Colombo*, berthed in 'stern-in' style at Genoa in a view dated 1954. (ALF collection)

Maiden call: dressed in flags, the 29,000grt *Cristoforo Colombo* arrives at Boston for the first time. (ALF collection)

lifted that forbade any new Italian passenger ships being built before 1955. Soon after those four survivors were restored, plans were laid for brand-new liners: big, fast and very luxurious. The 27,000-ton sisters *Giulio Cesare* and *Augustus* came first, however, in 1951–52, for the pressing South Atlantic run, between Italy, Brazil, Uruguay and Argentina. The intended pair for the all-important northern trade to New York were to be bigger and better still.

'The *Andrea Doria* and her sister, the *Cristoforo Colombo*, introduced new concepts in design, had stylish interiors and used the best names in Italian art and decoration,' reported Maurizio Eliseo, also one of Italy's finest maritime scholars and the author of several books about ocean liners:

To many appraisers, the 23-knot *Andrea Doria* and her sister ship were two of the very best-looking liners of the 1950s. (ALF collection)

Tragedy: the sinking *Andrea Doria* on the morning of 26 July 1956. (ALF collection)

The 680ft-long *Augustus* at Pier 84, New York, in a view dated 1957. (ALF collection)

Far left: Strolling: the enclosed promenade deck aboard the *Giulio Cesare*. (Italian Line)

Left: Post-war moderne: the first-class main lounge aboard the *Giulio Cesare*. (Italian Line)

It was said at the time that the *Andrea Doria* was a 'ship built like an oil on canvas, with parts of the greatest artists coming together'. Some of her artworks were in fact inspired by the Renaissance, the great master artists, and of course she was the symbol of another renaissance, the Italian maritime renaissance of the late 1940s and '50s. Alone, she was a great symbol.

A three-class ship that could carry up to 1,248 passengers, the 23-knot *Doria* was built at Genoa, by the Ansaldo shipyard. She was launched in June 1951 and then commissioned, for a short cruise from Genoa to the Canaries and back, in December 1952. 'She was an outstanding ship when completed. Everyone was very pleased with her,' added Eliseo:

On her maiden voyage, the *Giulio Cesare* prepares to sail from Trieste. (ALF collection)

She was, after all, the first North Atlantic liner built in Italy since the 1930s. She was also said to be very advanced. Her safety, for example, was assured not only by the Italians, but by the Americans and the British as well. She was actually said to be one of the safest ships afloat. Safety was paramount at the time for the Italians. They wanted especially to revive their fine shipbuilding reputation from before the war. Earlier, the *Rex* and *Conte di Savoia* had been the very first ships to comply with the SOLAS [Safety of Life at Sea] standards of 1929. The *Doria* complied with the newer standards, amended in 1948.

But the fates were cruel to the glorious 29,000-ton *Doria*. On a foggy summer's night, 25 July 1956, she was rammed off Nantucket island by a Swedish American liner, the 12,500-ton *Stockholm*. The westbound Italian ship was mortally wounded. While the badly damaged Swede limped back to New York, the abandoned pride of Italy rolled over on her side and sank in the early daylight of the next morning. She was gone, over fifty people had perished and a long court battle over responsibility followed (it was, in fact, never settled).

'It was really a national funeral when the *Doria* was lost,' reported Maurizio Eliseo:

> It was like seeing the dream of post-war Italy turn into a nightmare. In Genoa, people cried in the streets, others stood weeping outside Italian Line headquarters and badly depressed dockers even refused to load ships. Within two days, the Italian Line, attempting to revive spirits, announced their plans for the *Leonardo da Vinci*. She would be bigger, faster, more beautiful, even more gorgeous.

6

'LIKE A BIG, WHITE YACHT': *KUNGSHOLM* (1953)

As the early morning fog gave way to bright sunshine in August 1984, we lined the upper, outer decks of P&O Cruises' *Sea Princess* as she arrived at Cádiz, Spain. The port and then the cityscape were before us. But as a team of tugs nudged into one of the longer berths, a great surprise was soon revealed. As I had been travelling for six weeks in Australia and then Indonesia, I had had little shipping news. Costa Cruises' *Columbus C* was just ahead, in the adjoining berth, but half-sunk at the pier, resting in the harbour mud and sitting about 20ft off the actual quayside. Oil booms surrounded her outer sides while most of her normally immaculate hull was scarred with great stains. There were even the first traces of rust. Her stern was low in the water, resting no more than 15ft above the murky waters of Cádiz harbour. The entire ship seemed lifeless, except for some laundry strung about the aft decks which perhaps belonged to her caretaker crew. She seemed a lost, very sad ship. At first, few of us aboard the *Sea Princess* had any knowledge of what had happened. There was, however, one notation to the day. As we were berthed stern to stern, I realised one fact: these two liners shared the same heritage. Both ships had belonged to the Swedish American Line and both had been named *Kungsholm*. The *Columbus C* had been the *Kungsholm* of 1953; the *Sea Princess* was her replacement, having been the *Kungsholm* of 1966.

Built at the De Schelde shipyards in Vlissingen, Holland, the 600ft-long *Kungsholm* was one of the gleaming symbols of a revitalised, post-war transatlantic liner trade. To a tug and fireboat reception, she sailed into New York Harbor for the first time on 3 December 1953. She was met by the outbound *Gripsholm*, a veteran liner dating from 1925, and then berthed at Swedish American's terminal, Pier 97 at the foot of West 57th Street. The visiting press and travel agent community was delighted with her. Everett Viez, an experienced agent as well as passenger ship traveller, noted, 'She was a good-sized liner, but more like a big, white yacht':

She had perfect proportions on the outside – two nicely raked funnels set between two masts, a sleek bow and curved stern. Everything seemed to work. Inside, she was glistening, cozy, welcoming, immaculate of course. She was indeed one of the most charming new liners of the 1950s and an immediate favorite with the New York travel set. Swedish American also had a high reputation in the cruise business, especially for long, luxurious cruises. Myself, I booked any number of clients on the Christmas–New Year cruises to the Caribbean of the *Kungsholm*, but also clients on the likes of the same ship's three-month-long cruises around-the-world.

Weighing in at 21,141 tons, the *Kungsholm* was not only the glistening new Swedish flagship, but also the very first big North Atlantic liner to boast of all outside cabins, no matter whether first or tourist class, and the first to have all staterooms with at least a private shower and toilet. (Cunard's big, new *Caronia*, commissioned in 1948, also had facilities in every cabin, but she was primarily marketed as a cruise ship and not an Atlantic liner.) Along with saunas and an indoor swimming pool (a portable outdoor pool was added for winter cruises to warm weather ports), she was decorated in a delightful, almost pre-war style of polished woods and fireplaces, and especially comfortable chairs and sofas. Indeed, she was noted for her 'club-like' atmosphere, which was especially useful when her passenger capacity was cut in half, from 842 to as few as 400 for long, luxurious, off-season cruises. Tremendously successful, she inspired a slightly larger version, a new *Gripsholm*, commissioned in 1957. She was built by the Italians at Genoa.

While the 19-knot, twin-screw *Kungsholm* made many summer-season crossings between Gothenburg, Copenhagen and New York, it was as a cruise ship that she won perhaps her greatest acclaim. Filled with millionaires, retired American corporate heads and even Hollywood stars, she went off in autumn on the likes of eight-week cruises to the Mediterranean or around continental South America. Alternate to her ninety-five-day circumnavigations, she might cruise around Africa. In the early 1960s, she began making an annual springtime cruise to the wine districts of Spain and western France, and to smaller, more remote ports in England, Wales and Scotland. But with a new, larger *Kungsholm* being constructed on the Clyde in the mid 1960s, the earlier *Kungsholm* was redundant and soon sold to North German Lloyd in late 1965. The Germans needed a replacement for their aged *Berlin*, which had been the earlier *Gripsholm*, dating from 1925.

Refitted at Bremerhaven, the *Kungsholm* was restyled as the *Europa* for a few Atlantic crossings, but mostly for cruises from New York, as well as Bremerhaven and Genoa. Her fleet mate was the larger *Bremen*, the former

Transatlantic crossings aboard Swedish American Line in 1961. (Author's collection)

Handsome and sparkling, the 600ft-long *Kungsholm* seen here in a night-time view at Pier 97, New York. (Port Authority of New York & New Jersey)

Refitted as the *Europa*, the former *Kungsholm* arrives at New York's Pier 88 for the first time under West German colours in January 1966. (Moran Towing & Transportation Co.)

French *Pasteur*. But when the *Bremen* was sold off (in late 1971) and after North German Lloyd merged with the Hamburg America Line to form Hapag-Lloyd, the *Europa* was repainted in all white and given new funnel colours for her full-time cruise schedules starting in September 1972. Then running almost exclusively with German passengers, she did indeed have a 'clubhouse' feel about her. Noted for her precision service and immaculate housekeeping, she attracted many regular passengers who came year after year. German millionaires, it was said, loved her.

The *Europa* was replaced, however, by a larger, more luxurious, purposely built new *Europa*, commissioned in late 1981. The older ship was sold to Costa Cruises, but in fact assigned to one of their holding companies, the Panama-registered Independent Continental Lines, and with the financial owner being Curaçao-registered Milestone. Expected to run West German charter cruises, she was cleverly renamed *Columbus C*, a reminder of sorts of the famed pre-war North German Lloyd liner *Columbus* of the 1920s and '30s. The *Columbus C*'s first Costa cruise departed Genoa on 18 December 1981, on a mid-Atlantic voyage to Buenos Aires and ports along the South American east coast. She later cruised the Mediterranean, Scandinavia (from Bremerhaven) and made several long cruises as well. Early in 1984, however, and as Costa was trimming its fleet, there was a rumour that the ship would be sold to the Chinese, who planned to run it as the *Friendship*. But further charter work kept her in European waters and it was during one of these voyages, on 29 July 1984, that she rammed the outer breakwater in high winds while arriving at Cádiz. Damaged, she began to flood and list. After being righted she finally sank upright at the pier. All of her engine spaces and lower passenger decks were badly flooded. Two months later, in September, she was declared a complete loss and ordered to be removed by Spanish authorities. In November, she was pumped out and raised by a Dutch salvage company. While there were reports that she was to be repaired, then towed to South Africa and afterward used as a hotel ship, the ex-*Kungsholm* was in fact sold for scrap, having been demolished at Barcelona (the port of Castellón had first been reported) in the spring of 1985.

7

MEDITERRANEAN FAVOURITE: *OLYMPIA* (1953)

'My parents and I left Greece, from the port of Piraeus, in June 1960 and we came to America, to New York, for the first time,' recalled Irene De Leonardis:

We actually lived in southern Rumania, but we are of Greek heritage. Just traveling down to Athens and to the port of Piraeus took 5 days. Of course, we seemed to have lots of luggage since we were leaving for good. My father's cousin had immigrated to America in 1939, just before the Second World War, and he had always encouraged us to follow. He promised that we would be happy in America. He offered my father a job and had even found us a small apartment in Brooklyn as a beginning. The 14-day crossing on the *Olympia* was the start, our first chapter. On the way, we stopped at Naples, Messina, Lisbon and Halifax. But the crossing of the Atlantic Ocean was often rough, the ship unsteady and I remember being quite ill. My parents brought food to me in our small cabin down in the bottom of the ship. I seemed to be in that room for several days, sick as well as afraid. I even feared the ship would sink and I would be separated from my parents. I was twelve at the time and it all seemed strange, so different, so unlike the home we had left behind.

There were many other Greeks on board as well, many of them moving to either to Canada or the United States. There were also some Greek–Americans aboard and who told many stories to the others, to the immigrants, about life in America. In ways, these talks were great preparations. It was fortunate that the stewards and waiters were all Greeks and so we could chat in our native language. My English was very limited then. My mother sometimes cried. She was quickly homesick. There was still family and, of course, many memories left behind in Rumania and in Greece itself.

Another very good-looking ship, the *Olympia* sails past the cliffs of Dover in her maiden year, 1953. (ALF collection)

Once we reached New York, it was a wonderful sight, seeing all of those tall buildings as the bright sun rose behind them. Those towers seemed to be shining, gleaming, like tops of a fairytale castle. I had heard of the Empire State Building and remember recognising it as we sailed up along the Hudson River. My father's cousin, his wife and two of their sons and their wives were waiting on Pier 88 for our arrival. After lunch, following long customs and immigration, we drove to Brooklyn. As we crossed the Brooklyn Bridge, I thought of the *Olympia*, the adventure of crossing the Atlantic Ocean and then beginning our new lives in the United States. I still have a deck of playing cards with a picture of the *Olympia* on each card. Now [1995] that my parents are dead, that deck of cards is the last link to that important part of our family history, that voyage to a new life.

Transocean comfort and relaxation on the Greek Line in advertising dated 1954. (Author's collection)

Another Greek Line advertisement, but dated 1962. (Author's collection)

April 1961: a record day for departing passengers at New York: (from top to bottom) *Hanseatic, Italia, Ocean Monarch, Queen of Bermuda, Sylvania, Lillevan* (a freighter chartered to Cunard) and the Onassis yacht *Christina, Flandre, Olympia, United States* and *Atlantic.* (Moran Towing & Transportation Co.)

The 22,979-ton *Olympia* was the pride of the Greek Line, beginning with her maiden Atlantic crossing in October 1953. She was immediately praised as one of the best-looking liners of the early 1950s. Built in Scotland, at the Alexander Stephen & Sons shipyard at Glasgow, she ranked as the very first newly built liner for a Greek company. Prior Greek passenger ships had always been bought second hand. The 611ft-long *Olympia* might have been called *Frederica*, honouring the Queen of Greece, but a regulatory dispute arose with the Greek Government before the ship's completion, the name was soon changed to *Olympia* and even her registry was switched to Liberia. But the tone of the ship remained Greek: Greek service, Greek food, Greek ambience. Typically, she was class-divided: as many as 138 could travel in small, select, upper-deck first class, while as many as 1,169 could go in less expensive tourist class. Many of her cabins had private bathrooms and there was a nice array of public rooms and facilities, including a lido area with two small swimming pools. In 1955, peak summer season fares for the twelve nights between Piraeus and New York ranged from $300 in first class to $178 in tourist class.

Rebuilt and modernised, the 611ft-long former *Olympia* but in her final career as the cruise ship *Regal Empress*. (ALF collection)

The *Olympia* made cruises in the winter months, the traditional slow season for Atlantic liners. She sailed the Caribbean, often on two-week itineraries, and also a luxurious, annual eight-week cruise around the Mediterranean and to Black Sea ports. In the late 1960s, having been joined by the larger *Queen Anna Maria* (the former *Empress of Britain*), the 21-knot *Olympia* also became popular for her three-day weekend cruises (Friday evening to Monday morning) from New York, so-called 'cruises to nowhere'. A relaxing, fun and party-filled weekend could cost as little as $75 per person.

The Greek Line fell on hard times by the mid 1970s, such that the *Olympia* was laid up (in Perama Bay, near Piraeus) in 1974 and then the *Queen Anna Maria* closed down the company a year later. After seven years, in quiet, backwater solitude, the *Olympia* was revived, however. In 1981, she was towed to Hamburg, refitted and re-engined (with diesels), to become the cruise ship *Caribe*, flying the Panamanian flag for Miami-based Commodore Cruise Lines. Largely rebuilt and modernised, her quarters were restyled for 1,160 passengers in 463 suites and cabins. Mostly, she cruised on seven-day itineraries out of Miami, usually sailing to eastern Caribbean ports.

In 1993, the *Caribe* was sold again, this time raising the house flag of Florida-based Regal Cruises and being re-christened *Regal Empress*. Her sailing range expanded, including a seasonal roster (June through September) of one- to twelve-day cruises from New York. Her winter base was Port Manatee, along Florida's west coast and near Tampa. She was quite popular and often filled to capacity, but one-ship operations such as Regal Cruises are very vulnerable to general conditions. In the spring of 2003, in the wake of struggling, deeply discounted trends following the terrorist attacks of 11 September 2001, Regal Cruises collapsed and the 50-year-old *Regal Empress* was seized for debts by local marshals and creditors. She did, however, find other buyers, Imperial Majesty Cruise Lines, based in Fort Lauderdale, for their immensely popular two-night cruise service between Port Everglades and Nassau. The ship soon had many loyal followers. The author once met a lady who so loved the *Regal Empress* that she sailed on it every month – twelve cruises a year! They also replaced another cruising veteran, the 48-year-old *Ocean Breeze* (ex-*Southern Cross*), which had been retired and sold to breakers in Bangladesh.

Ageing ships are increasingly expensive – and increasingly problematic, however. While she appeared in the TV series *Mythbusters*, the *Regal Empress* found a lucrative charter in September 2008 – to serve as a relief ship in Texas for victims of disastrous Hurricane Ike. She returned to service in December, but all too briefly. In March 2009, she was retired, being replaced by the larger, more modern *Bahamas Celebration*, a converted Norwegian ferry. The 56-year-old *Regal Empress* was sent over to Freeport in the Bahamas, laid up and awaiting sale. Only Indian scrap merchants were seriously interested, however, and she was sold within a month, in April. Promptly, the old liner set off on the long, slow, three-month voyage to India, to the beaches of Alang. She arrived and was beached on 24 July. Demolition began in October and she was gone completely within two and half months.

8

ARCADIA AND NEW P&O TONNAGE TO THE EAST (1954)

After the North Atlantic run between Europe and North America, one of the busiest ocean liner routes was between the UK and Australia. Like the North Atlantic, it was supported by a regular passenger trade, but also had a huge backbone: a seemingly unlimited, outbound, low-fare immigrant trade. One of Britain's most famous, most historic shipping companies, the Peninsular & Oriental Steam Navigation Company Limited (P&O) was heavily (and profitably) involved for decades in this now all-but-gone Australian liner service. In 1960, they were merged with another London-based company, the Orient Line, and used no less than twelve large passenger ships at their peak. P&O-Orient Lines, as they were called until 1966 (before reverting to the simpler P&O name), had regular sailings to Australia, but also on worldwide itineraries that included over 100 ports in the Middle East, the Far East, North America and the Caribbean.

After considerable losses during the destructive years of the Second World War, both the P&O and Orient lines constructed a large list of new liners: *Orcades* (1948), *Himalaya* (1949), *Chusan* (1950), *Oronsay* (1951), *Arcadia* (1954), *Iberia* (1954), *Orsova* (1955) and finally the larger and faster *Oriana* (1960) and *Canberra* (1961).

The 721ft-long *Arcadia*, built on Scotland's River Clyde by the famed John Brown & Company Limited, was among the most popular ships of this combined P&O-Orient fleet. Her near sister, the *Iberia*, never quite had the same popularity or success. She was a troubled ship in several ways. Weighing in at 29,734 tons, the *Arcadia* carried some 1,390 passengers – 655 in first class and up to 735 in tourist class. The passengers were almost evenly divided between a pleasant, very comfortable first class and a simpler, almost austere and less expensive first class. Her line voyages were often expanded to a round-the-world itinerary. One *Arcadia* voyage amounted to 120 days in total and read: Southampton to Gibraltar, Naples, Piraeus, Suez, Aden, Bombay, Colombo, Fremantle, Melbourne, Sydney, Singapore, Hong Kong,

Kobe, Yokohama Honolulu, Vancouver, San Francisco, Los Angeles, Acapulco, the Panama Canal, Curaçao, Fort Lauderdale, Nassau, Bermuda and finally a return to Southampton. Fares in the early 1960s ranged from $15 per person and up in first class to $9 and up in tourist class. Some passengers made the full, four-month-long trip, while others sailed outward to Australia and still others made short two- to seven-night passages between ports.

Tony Ralph, a keen ship enthusiast from New Zealand and former cruise liner staff member, recalled his very first P&O cruise, aboard the *Arcadia*, in 1966. It was a short cruise from Auckland to Pitcairn and Tin Can islands. 'She was a great ship with a colonial country club style,' he remembered. 'She was lighter in style and decor than, say, the earlier *Himalaya*. The *Arcadia* got away from the traditional dark woods favoured by P&O for their earlier passenger ships. There was indirect lighting and ceiling designs on board the *Arcadia* as well.'

Life on board in the 1960s was quite different, as Tony Ralph remembers, from today's hotel-like, activity-filled cruise ships:

Daily life on P&O liners, even in the 1960s, had its rituals. These rituals were part of P&O's sea-going culture. A cup of tea and a biscuit was served each morning to all passengers in their cabins, for example. This was a pre-breakfast tradition. Lunch was always offered in the restaurant, down on B Deck, whereas a buffet lunch on the open deck was considered an event and might be offered only once during an entire cruise. Everyone was very punctual at meal times, especially at dinner. Travel by ship, even in the 1960s, was still very special to Australians and New Zealanders. Yes, it was all very ritualised.

On the *Arcadia*, after dinner in the restaurant, coffee was served in the lounge and it was very much a separate event. There were lots of conversational areas in the lounges and so you met more passengers over the course of the voyage. Formal entertainment was minimal. A film was the only offering some nights.

Fanfare: launching day, 14 May 1953, for P&O's 721ft-long *Arcadia*. (P&O)

The 29,000grt *Arcadia* was indeed an imposing ship, the largest and finest on the UK–Australia run in the mid 1950s. (ALF collection)

Then there was an Easter Parade of Hats, Frog Racing and Tombola on others. Cabaret shows were unheard of back then, but a big, high-spirited disco on an aft, open deck was a big, well-attended event! There was no television or even radio in the cabins on the *Arcadia* so that reading the printed daily news sheets was also an activity.

Captain Nick Carlton also remembered the 22-knot, steam-turbine-driven *Arcadia*. He served on her in the mid 1970s:

We made the ship's last Vancouver to Sydney line voyage in preparation for the ship being based full-time in Australia for full-time, one-class cruising. She was a lovely, very traditional ship. We would have two- and three-day layovers in some ports, but once at sea, we often ran at high speeds and burned huge amounts of fuel. Actually, there was lots of excess spending in those days. P&O ran the bars and the bingo – and so there was lots of theft by the crew. There was still full Union crews at the time, wages were high and some cabin stewards received such massive tips from passengers that they actually flew home in mid

voyage. Ships like the *Arcadia* were also very solid, very strong. We will never see that standard of construction again.

The *Iberia*, always the more troublesome of the pair, went to the breakers prematurely, in 1972. She was just 18 years old. There was massive airline competition for P&O by then as well as increased fuel oil and staff costs, the loss of cargo to containerships and generally ageing ships. The other P&O liners soon went to the scrappers as well. The *Arcadia*, finishing her days as a Sydney-based cruise ship, endured the longest of the late 1940s/early 1950s group. She finally ended her days, at age 25, in 1979 at a Taiwanese scrap yard.

Liners such as the two-class *Arcadia* also had considerable cargo capacities, transported in six holds. (P&O)

The *Arcadia* is seen here at Vancouver, during an around-the-world cruise. (P&O)

9

CUNARD TO THE ST LAWRENCE: *SAXONIA & IVERNIA* (1954–55)

Cunard Line's *Saxonia* and *Ivernia* were ships of the mid 1950s. They were the first of a quartet of popular transatlantic liners, but less for Cunard's celebrated service to and from New York than for the company's alternative service to Montreal and Québec City. Commissioned in September 1954 and July 1955, these 608ft-long ships were later extensively refitted and began

separate Cunard careers, beginning in 1963 as the *Carmania* and *Franconia*. Both had long lives – approximately fifty years for each ship.

Created by the famed John Brown shipyard at Clydebank in Scotland, the master builders of such legendary liners as the *Lusitania*, *Aquitania*, *Queen Mary*, *Queen Elizabeth* and *QE2*, they were actually first intended to be a

With her distinctive domed funnel, the 22,000-grt *Saxonia* represented a new generation of Cunarders. (Cunard Line)

pair of sisters, but an order later extended to four. The other, later ships were the *Carinthia* of 1956 and the *Sylvania* of 1957. At just under 22,000 tons, they were passenger liners that had, for added revenue, good-sized cargo capacities as well – three hatches forward and three aft. Steamships with top speeds of some 20 knots, the twin-screw *Saxonia* and *Ivernia* were used on the Cunard run between London or Southampton, Le Havre, Cobh, Québec City and Montreal, but only between April and December. In winter, when the St Lawrence was clogged with ice, the two sailed to Halifax and then to New York, where they tended to remain in port for five or six days. Carrying around 110 in first class and as many as 830 in tourist class, they catered to general passenger traffic, the tourist business and, going westbound to Canada, the immigrant trade. In the 1950s until the early '60s, many Britons in particular sought new lives in Canada.

'We left London in 1960 and crossed to Canada on the *Saxonia*,' recalled Mrs Aviva Greenberg:

My parents decided that we could have a better life with more opportunity, especially for our future, in Canada and so we decided to move to Toronto and later to Calgary. I do not recall the specifics of the *Saxonia* crossing, but we left Southampton on a dark November day, as I remember. It was very common in those days to sail across, but seeking the lowest passage rates and the dates that worked. It was low season for fares. The cost was $150 each. My father and mother had saved enough money for the four of us, my brother included, to make the journey. Ships were ideal for extra luggage and then were of course much cheaper than the airlines. In 1960, to cross by air was quite expensive – a luxury. On the voyage, there were others like us, who were moving to Canada, and so this made the sense of parting easier. Myself, I recall being very excited about the whole experience, especially the first day in Montreal and then the train ride to our new home near Toronto.

Tugs assist the arriving *Saxonia* at Montreal. (ALF collection)

The *Saxonia* and *Ivernia* were made over as cruise ships during extended refits at the John Brown yard at Clydebank in 1962–63. (Cunard Line)

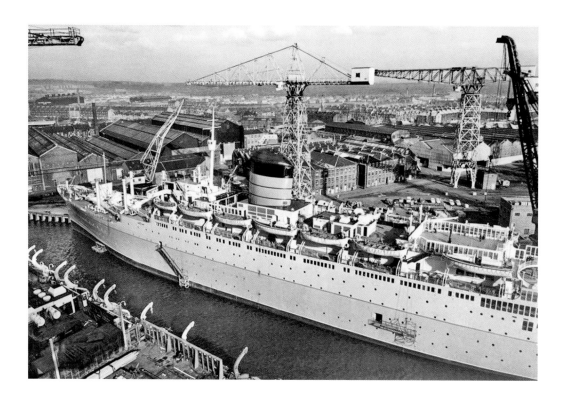

When the *Saxonia* and *Ivernia* were renamed *Carmania* and *Franconia* in 1963, they were repainted in several shades of green, Cunard's so-called 'cruising green'. They were extensively refitted with aft lido decks, an outdoor pool, full air conditioning and bathroom facilities for all cabins. Their Atlantic crossings were hereafter extended to include Rotterdam, but limited to about six months of the year. The remainder of the year was for Caribbean cruises – the *Carmania* departing from Port Everglades, Florida, and the *Franconia* from New York. Later, as the Atlantic trade fell away, declining in the face of airline competition that had become more affordable, both ships became year-round cruise ships. The *Carmania* divided her time between winters in Florida and the remainder from Southampton; the *Franconia* did wintertime Florida service alternating with, from April to November, six-day cruises between New York and Bermuda (minimum fare in 1967 was $165).

Cunard retired these two ships in 1971 and then sold them two years later to the Soviets, more specifically to the Odessa-based Black Sea Steamship Company. Now bearing the hammer and sickle on their domed funnels, the former *Saxonia/Carmania* was renamed *Leonid Sobinov* while the ex-*Ivernia/Franconia* changed to *Feodor Shalyapin*. They were often used for western charters (usually to the London-based CTC Lines), cruising from Britain, Germany, Italy and even far-off Australia. They also made occasional line voyages from Southampton to Sydney or the reverse and, for their Soviet owners, carried soldiers, technicians and even sports teams to East Africa, the Middle East and to Cuba. After the collapse of the Soviet Union in 1991, they hoisted the Maltese flag through separate owning companies. But monies were sparse, repairs were needed and the two ships became rundown and tired.

Both ships were laid up by 1996, with rumours that investors would see to extensive refits and reactivation for both of them. This never happened, however. The *Sobinov* was sold to India for scrapping in April 1999 while the *Shalyapin* lingered for a time at Ilyichevsk, a Black Sea naval port, until sold to breakers in the winter of 2004.

10

REVOLUTIONARY DESIGN: *SOUTHERN CROSS* (1955)

In August 2003, following a slow voyage from Freeport in the Bahamas via the Mediterranean and Suez, the liner *Ocean Breeze* finally reached remote Chittagong in Bangladesh. She was not on a cruise or any voyage even remotely commercial, but on her very last passage. She would soon be run aground deliberately on the local beaches and then invaded by small armies of scrap and demolition crews. The 48-year-old passenger ship was ending a long, interesting and often noteworthy career. While she had also been the *Calypso* and then the *Azure Seas*, she is perhaps best remembered as one of Britain's finest ocean liners of the post-Second World War era, Shaw Savill Line's *Southern Cross*.

When Queen Elizabeth II named the 20,000-ton ship at her launching in August 1954, she was another distinguished product of the great Harland & Wolff shipyard at Belfast in Northern Ireland. From the same slipways came the likes of the *Olympic* and her immortal sister *Titanic*, the *Statendam* of 1929, the last White Star liners *Britannic* and *Georgic*, the celebrated cruise ship *Andes* and the P&O flagship *Canberra*. The *Southern Cross* was the first brand-new liner in the Shaw Savill fleet since the *Dominion Monarch*, commissioned in 1939 but actually from a Harland & Wolff rival, Swan Hunter's yard at Newcastle.

The 604ft-long *Southern Cross* was a totally different passenger ship, something of a revolutionary, and the result of extensive research. She was, for example, the first large liner to have her funnel mounted aft therefore freeing the midships section for passenger areas, pools and open-air sections. This layout was later copied by many other passenger ship designers. She was also the first all-tourist-class liner, carrying 1,100 at capacity and in cabins from upper-deck singles to economical four- and six-berth rooms on the lower decks. There were no class divisions on the *Southern Cross*. Passengers had full run of the ship. Furthermore, she was the first pure passenger liner in that she carried no cargo whatsoever other than passenger baggage and some mail. Finally, unlike other British liners serving Australia, the 20-knot *Southern Cross* was routed on continuous ten-week trips around the world: Southampton to South Africa, then across to Australia and New Zealand, then northward to Panama and the Caribbean before returning to the UK, or the same routing but in reverse. A very popular ship from the start, she carried British migrants to Australia, Australians going to Britain and Europe on extended budget holidays and the occasional tourist, some making the full world voyage as a sort of a cruise, and inter-port passenger. She was so successful that, a near sister, the somewhat larger *Northern Star*, was added to the Shaw Savill fleet in 1962.

'We had mainly immigrants on board the *Southern Cross*, even well into the 1960s,' noted Jim Clench, then an engineer at Shaw Savill:

In the 1950s and '60s, many UK people were seeking a better life elsewhere and went to Australia House in London to apply for a fare-assisted passage Down Under. They waited. It was, after all, a ten-pound fare for the six-week voyage from Southampton to Fremantle, Melbourne or Sydney. Many people in the UK saw Australia as a palm tree-lined paradise. They did not see the harsh reality.

'The orchestra was the only entertainment on board the *Southern Cross*,' added Clench:

There was also a little jazz band in the ship's bar-pub and a disco girl for records. The purser was the cruise director. Few cabins had private bathroom facilities and there were two dining rooms with two sittings for each meal. The British immigrants going to Australia could not wait for meal times. Some had never been served by a waiter in their lives and often were quite demanding, even rude to the staff. Coming home to Southampton, we would have about 1,000 passengers aboard, about 90% of capacity. There would be returning immigrants, who had done well in Australia, as well as Australian back-packers. They were 'real passengers', in a better mood, with a different outlook and purpose to their voyage, and they even gave tips. The crew was in better spirits as well. Of course, we had an all-British crew on board. Basically, Shaw Savill Line was a cargo company that had some passenger ships whereas P&O-Orient, our greatest rival, was a passenger company with some cargo ships.

'There were two other notations about the *Southern Cross*,' concluded Jim Clench. 'The engineers' quarters on board was the only space on the ship that was not air conditioned. The Shaw Savill superintendent feared the engineers would catch cold and therefore voyages could be disrupted, even delayed. Also, and like all Shaw Savill ships of that period, the *Southern Cross* smelled of buttermilk soap. It was a special variety used by both passengers and crew, and the smell permeated the entire ship.'

By 1971, the Australian and around-the-world liner trades for ships such as the 16-year-old *Southern Cross* were falling away. Airline competition was the greatest blow. She was soon laid up, then offered for sale. However, while she might have gone prematurely to the scrap yard, the ship found further life

Comparison in size: the 20,200-ton *Southern Cross* at Wellington with another Union Line passenger ship, the 6,100-ton *Rangatira* on the right. (ALF collection)

The innovative, 1,100-passenger *Southern Cross* berthed at Wellington – with Union Line's *Maori* on the right. (ALF collection)

with the Greeks. Sailing for the Ulysses Line, she re-emerged in 1973 as the refitted, modernised *Calypso* and ran mostly charter cruises until sold again, in 1979, to Western Cruise Lines, who then sailed her mostly on the US west coast as the *Azure Seas*. Western was a sister company to Miami-based Eastern Cruise Lines, which ran the *Emerald Seas* (ex-*Laguardia*, ex-*Leilani*, etc.), but which sailed between Florida and the Bahamas.

In 1992, the *Azure Seas* was sold again, this time to the Dolphin Cruise Lines, also Florida-based, who renamed her as *Ocean Breeze*. She then ran mostly Caribbean itineraries, sailing from Aruba as well as Port Everglades and Miami. In 2000, while continuing under the name *Ocean Breeze*, she began sailing on two-night cruises between Port Everglades and Nassau for Imperial Majesty Cruise Lines.

It seems, however, that by the spring of 2003, old age had caught up with the former Shaw Savill liner. Regal Cruises, which had slipped into bankruptcy, had their *Regal Empress* on the auction block. Although slightly older, dating from 1953, when she was completed as the Greek *Olympia*, she was actually in better condition and so replaced the then tired *Ocean Breeze*. Soon after her final cruise to Nassau, the ex-*Southern Cross* was sold to Indian and then resold to Bangladeshi scrap merchants, thereby concluding a long and interesting life.

This woman is a sailor

This charming sailor wouldn't know a square-knot from a bowline and to her a "sharp watch" is a smart piece of jewelry that ticks. But it takes sailors of every specialty to run the great sunliner Constitution and Ruth Gallo is tops in her field. She's the ship's Social Directress, and it's her job to see that everybody's happy. A specialist in the "Boy meets Girl" department, this gay match-maker has more than one happy marriage to her credit.

It's her delight to organize costume balls, children's parties, talent shows, cocktail parties or anything else you want. Does she make the Constitution a happy place to be? Well, every year guests return again and again, and many make round trips without getting off the ship.

It's sailors like Ruth who have earned the Constitution and Independence that highest seagoing accolade . . . "Happy Ships."

SEE YOUR TRAVEL AGENT OR
AMERICAN EXPORT LINES
39 BROADWAY, NEW YORK 6, N. Y.

THE SUNLANE TO EUROPE | INDEPENDENCE · CONSTITUTION ☆ EXCALIBUR · EXCAMBION · EXOCHORDA · EXETER
GIBRALTAR, CANNES, GENOA, NAPLES · FRANCE, ITALY, EGYPT, LEBANON, SYRIA, TURKEY, GREECE, SPAIN

HOLIDAY/JANUARY

Art disco: the short-lived mod sunburst effect for the *Independence* in 1968. The *Oceanic* is on the right. (ALF collection)

Broken in half and aground, the very sad, former *Independence* off Alang in India in 2008. (Author's collection)

The evocative poster for the new *Ryndam* and *Maasdam*, dated 1953. (Norman Knebel collection)

A grand poster highlighting the maiden voyage of the *Giulio Cesare* in October 1951. (Norman Knebel collection)

Designer Wayne Mazzotta's depiction of the *Andrea Doria* taking on board an advanced Chrysler automobile at Genoa. (Wayne Mazzotta collection)

'Floating Riviera': advertising for the brand-new *Cristoforo Colombo* in 1954. (Author's collection)

Christmas Eve gathering at Genoa for the Italian Line in 1954 – the *Cristoforo Colombo* (left), *Vulcania*, *Conte Grande*, *Giulio Cesare* and *Andrea Doria*. (Italian Line)

"ITALIA"
SOCIETA' DI NAVIGAZIONE

AMERIQUES, PACIFIQUE NORD SUD

 In the early morning light on 26 July 1956, the listing *Andrea Doria* nears her tragic end. (ALF collection)

 Looking aft from the bow aboard the 680ft-long *Giulio Cesare*. (Author's collection)

 A splendid Italian Line poster of the 1950s. (Norman Knebel collection)

The *Augustus* and *Giulio Cesare* featured on the cover of *Power Ships*, the journal of the Steamship Historical Society of America, for their autumn 2012 edition. (Steamship Historical Society of America)

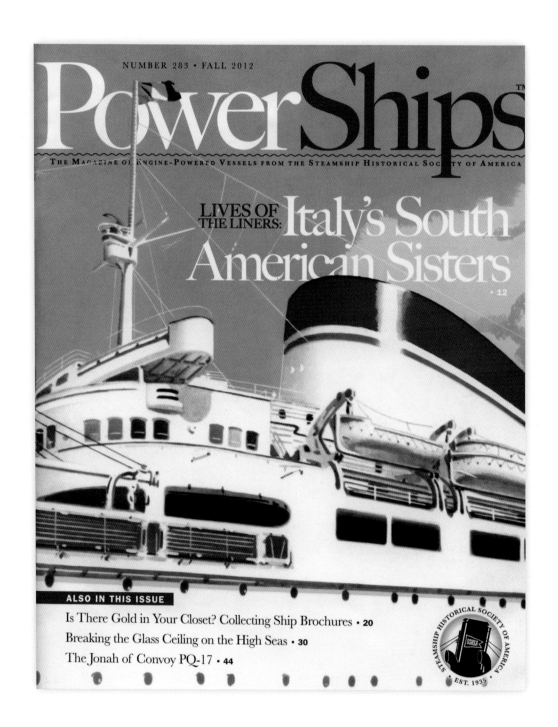

NUMBER 283 • FALL 2012

PowerShips™

THE MAGAZINE OF ENGINE-POWERED VESSELS FROM THE STEAMSHIP HISTORICAL SOCIETY OF AMERICA

LIVES OF
THE LINERS: Italy's South
American Sisters
• 12

ALSO IN THIS ISSUE

Is There Gold in Your Closet? Collecting Ship Brochures • **20**

Breaking the Glass Ceiling on the High Seas • **30**

The Jonah of Convoy PQ-17 • **44**

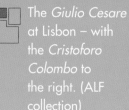
The *Giulio Cesare* at Lisbon – with the *Cristoforo Colombo* to the right. (ALF collection)

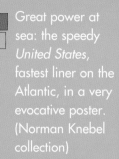
Great power at sea: the speedy *United States*, fastest liner on the Atlantic, in a very evocative poster. (Norman Knebel collection)

The former *Augustus* but seen in her final years as the *Philippines*, moored at Manila. (Peter Knego collection)

Created in the early 1960s, French artist Albert Brenet's depiction of the *United States*. The 990ft-long liner had the largest funnels afloat. (Moran Towing & Transportation Co.)

Outbound at Southampton: with the migrant ship *New Australia* on the right. (ALF collection)

Another stirring poster of the mighty *United States*. (Norman Knebel collection)

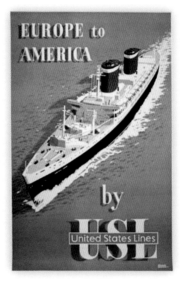

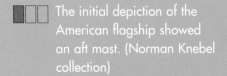 The initial depiction of the American flagship showed an aft mast. (Norman Knebel collection)

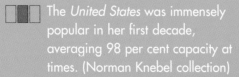 The *United States* was immensely popular in her first decade, averaging 98 per cent capacity at times. (Norman Knebel collection)

 Some passengers reported that the five-day crossings on board the *United States* were, in fact, all too brief. (Norman Knebel collection)

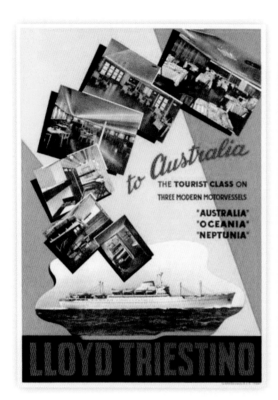

The three Lloyd Triestino sisters were said to be among the finest, best-served liners on the Australian run in the early 1950s. (Norman Knebel collection)

The *Australia* – shown at Melbourne – and her sisters carried up to 600 passengers in three classes as built. (ALF collection)

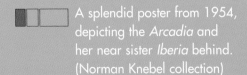 A splendid poster from 1954, depicting the *Arcadia* and her near sister *Iberia* behind. (Norman Knebel collection)

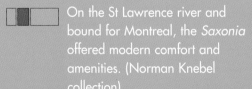 On the St Lawrence river and bound for Montreal, the *Saxonia* offered modern comfort and amenities. (Norman Knebel collection)

 The smart-looking *Southern Cross* made continuous seventy-six-night trips around the world. (Tim Noble collection)

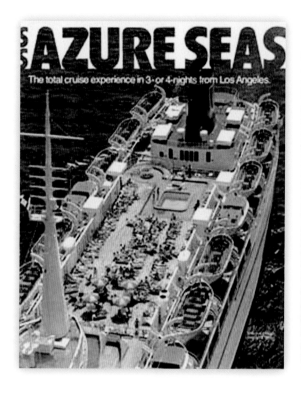

The *Southern Cross* in her later career as the cruise ship *Azure Seas*. (Norman Knebel collection)

Two fine liners of the 1950s were the 365-passenger converted freighters *Mariposa* and *Monterey*. They sailed between California, Hawaii and the South Pacific. (Norman Knebel collection)

Relaxation on long voyages: France's Chargeurs Réunis offered passenger services to South America, West Africa and South-east Asia. (Norman Knebel collection)

Starlit nights on the Furness-Bermuda Lines' *Ocean Monarch*. (Norman Knebel collection)

Crossing the Pacific on the big American President liners *President Cleveland* and *President Wilson*. (Norman Knebel collection)

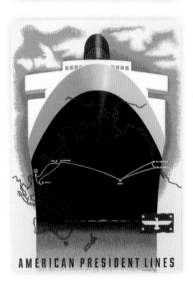

Shipboard safety and security is highlighted in this Chargeurs Réunis poster from 1952. (Norman Knebel collection)

Off to North and West Africa aboard the French Line, the Compagnie Générale Transatlantique (CGT). (Author's collection)

To eastern waters aboard the *Cambodge, Laos* and *Viet-Nam* of the French-flag Messageries Maritimes. (Author's collection)

Off to Matadi in the Congo aboard the new *Baudouinville* of Compagnie Maritime Belge, 1956–57. (Author's collection)

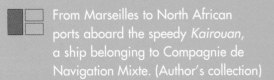 From Marseilles to North African ports aboard the speedy *Kairouan*, a ship belonging to Compagnie de Navigation Mixte. (Author's collection)

 The *Gripsholm* at Pier 97, New York – with a visiting French aircraft carrier just to the left. (Norman Knebel collection)

 During a summer cruise: the *Gripsholm* is brightly lit for an overnight call at Hamburg. (Author's collection)

S.S. JERUSALEM
Sistership of s.s. Theodor Herzl
FRANCE · ITALY · GREECE · CYPRUS · ISRAEL

Dressed in flags during a cruise, the *Cabo San Roque* and her sister were Spain's largest and finest passenger ships of the 1950s. (ALF collection)

Inter-Mediterranean services aboard the new *Jerusalem*, 1957–58. (Norman Knebel collection)

Late 1950s decor aboard the luxurious *Rotterdam*. (ALF collection)

The new *Rotterdam* in a 1959 maiden season poster. (Norman Knebel collection)

 Moored in Rotterdam harbour as a museum, hotel and reception centre, the magnificent *Rotterdam* makes for a striking evening addition to the port. (ALF collection)

A testament to the great age of 1950s ocean liners, the preserved *Rotterdam* as she appeared in 2015. (ALF collection)

11

BOUND FOR SOUTH AMERICA: *REINA DEL MAR* (1956)

The 20,500-ton *Reina Del Mar* was one of Britain's finest passenger liners built in the 1950s. A product of the illustrious Harland & Wolff shipyard at Belfast, the three-class steamship (750 berths in all) was in fact a historic liner as well: she was the very last British liner to serve on the long-haul route from Liverpool across to the Caribbean and Panama, and then along the entire west coast of South America. Completed in 1956, she actually sailed on that route for only seven years, until 1963, when the unbeatable airlines took almost all of her remaining passengers. She was soon transferred to another British liner company, Union-Castle, and was refitted for an increasingly more profitable venue in passenger shipping: one-class cruising. The *Reina Del Mar* continued as a very popular cruise ship until, in the face of rising fuel oil prices as well as operational costs, she was sold off to Taiwanese scrappers in 1975. The 601ft-long ship had barely reached 20 years of age.

'I joined Pacific Steam Navigation Company, commonly known as PSNC, when they were just retiring the 28-year-old *Reina Del Pacifico*, the predecessor to the then brand-new *Reina Del Mar*,' recalled Michael Stephen Peters, who went on to become chief engineer on the *Reina Del Mar*. Peters had started three years earlier, in 1955, in the then huge British merchant service, first

The maiden voyage for the 20,234-ton *Reina Del Mar*, seen on the River Mersey in May 1956. Elder Dempster's *Aureol* is on the far left, berthed at the Princes Landing Stage. (Pacific Steam Navigation Co. Ltd)

The *Reina Del Mar* (left) and the older *Reina Del Pacifico* meet at Callao in Peru in a view from 1957. (Pacific Steam Navigation Co. Ltd)

with the Shaw Savill Line, then New Zealand Shipping Company and with Elders & Fyffes before joining Liverpool-based Pacific Steam in 1958. 'The *Reina Del Pacifico* was near her end when I joined. She was having engine troubles in those final days and was operating on 3½ instead of 4 engines. I was soon posted to some of the Company freighters,' he added.

Peters joined the 20-knot *Reina Del Mar* in 1960–61 and has fond memories of that all-white liner that was topped off by a single, tapered, all-yellow funnel:

We were still doing five line voyages a year, sailing from Liverpool and then via La Rochelle, Santander and Vigo before crossing to Bermuda, Nassau, Kingston, Cartagena, the Panama Canal and then west coast of South America ports such as Guayaquil, Callao and Valparaiso. She was a good sea boat, but you needed to 'understand' her. Like all ships, she had her moods. We had mostly businessmen in first class and who often turned the long voyage into their holiday. We carried mostly immigrants in third class, usually from French

and Spanish ports, going to South America. In January, we often had passengers who took the ten-week round voyage as a complete cruise. It was an escape from the dreary British winters. We included ports such as Tenerife, Madeira, Barbados and Curacao on these voyages.

Like most passenger liners of that period, the *Reina Del Mar* also carried cargo. 'Cargo was good for extra revenue as well as ballast,' said Peters. 'We took mostly manufactured goods out from Liverpool as well as specialty food items, which were destined for hotels in the Caribbean and South America. On the homeward trips, we carried tin ore and Bolivian copper as well as fish meal and cotton.'

The airlines were merciless in their competitive battle with traditional passenger ship companies like Pacific Steam Navigation. Peters noted:

It was the sudden lack of passengers that killed the *Reina Del Mar*. Her demise on the South American run came quickly, in fact very quickly. Corporate thinking had changed and their executives and staff members could now do a one-day flight instead of a five or six week voyage. And the cargo we carried was better suited to freighters. The *Reina Del Mar* was quite empty in the end, carrying less than 50% of her capacity on some voyages. We experimented with one Mediterranean cruise, but cruising was not in Pacific Steam's thinking. She was soon chartered and then sold outright to the Union Castle Line for cruising. She also did some early cruising for TSA, the Travel Savings Association, a bargain operation that made cruises a sort of interest on banking. I recall that, in 1964, the *Reina Del Mar* was sent over to New York for the World's Fair. The two-week trips under TSA cost as little as 60 pounds [approximately $275 then].

In 1972, Michael Peters was made redundant in the great downsizing of the British merchant fleet and soon went ashore to work in the hotel business. When we met some thirty years later, on a Canadian cruise aboard the *Queen Elizabeth 2*, he still felt very nostalgic and sentimental when speaking of those bygone golden days of British shipping and specifically British ocean liners. 'I feel great sadness in seeing the great British fleet gone,' he said. 'We shall never see anything like it again.'

12

THE SUPERB *GRIPSHOLM* (1957)

In September 1957, the American news magazine *Newsweek* ran a cover story highlighting a boom in ocean liner travel on the North Atlantic. It was indeed a banner year. Several brand-new ships were featured – Cunard's *Sylvania*, Canadian Pacific's *Empress of England*, Holland America's *Statendam*, Zim Lines' *Jerusalem* and the *Gripsholm* of Swedish American Line. That beautiful Swede was one of the most handsome liners of her day.

Decades later, in the mid 1990s, the story was quite different. 'She had been in rather poor condition while lying in a quiet backwater at Tampa,' reported a London-based shipbroker friend. 'The former *Gripsholm* had been out of service for five years, ever since the collapse of her last owners, Regency Cruises, which closed down in October 1995. Thereafter, there were constant rumours that she would be scrapped.' But in July 2000, in the wake of other rumours that she would go to Stockholm and made over to be a combination floating hotel and cruise terminal, she sank off the South African coast while empty and being towed to Indian shipbreakers. Just before, to add to her final indignities, she had been raided by 'pirates' off West Africa and stripped of even her least valuable parts and machinery. A sad, much neglected and plundered ship, she began to flood and sank weeks later, on 12 July, while in heavy seas off Algoa in South Africa. Her career had been quite diverse, having been the Swedish *Gripsholm* and later the Greek *Navarino* and *Regent Sea*.

Built at Genoa, Italy, in 1957 (and on the same slip occupied by the likes of the *Andrea Doria*), the 631ft-long ship was launched by Sweden's Princess Margaretha as the *Gripsholm* for the Swedish American Line. She was not only one of the most handsome-looking liners then afloat, but one of the best run. 'In 1950s travel circles, the *Gripsholm* and her fleetmate *Kungsholm* [built 1953] were said to be like "big yachts",' recalled the late Everett Viez, a liner historian and travel agent. 'They were not only beautiful looking ships, but they were also superbly decorated, always immaculate and offered perfect

service as well as cuisine. To cross or cruise on these Swedish American liners was always a highlight.'

The *Gripsholm* sailed for a few months each year on the North Atlantic run, between Gothenburg, Copenhagen and New York, and carried up to 762 passengers. Her capacity was divided between 150 in posh, upper-deck first class and about 612 in less expensive, but extremely comfortable, tourist class (even the least expensive cabin had a private shower and toilet, for example). But for the rest of the year, from October through to April, her configuration was reduced to a clubby 450, all first class, as she made continuous cruises. Mostly, she made long, luxurious trips, all of them from New York, such as the Mediterranean and Black Seas (fifty-seven days), around South America (forty-nine days) and, as the ultimate voyage, around the world (ninety-five days). Her world cruise of 1965, as an example, was priced from $3,200 or little more than $30 per person per day. In summer,

The height of maritime modernity: the fully air-conditioned, stabilised *Gripsholm* was launched at Genoa on 8 April 1956. (Swedish American Line)

With each liner returned from holiday cruises to the Caribbean, New York's Luxury Liner Row in early January 1960: (from top to bottom) the *Homeric* departing and then, at berth, the *Gripsholm*, *Ocean Monarch*, *Italia*, *Queen Elizabeth*, *Mauretania* and *Berlin*. (Photofest)

she would also cruise to the North Cape and Scandinavia (forty-five days). Occasionally, she would run a twelve-day August cruise up to the Canadian Maritimes and the St Lawrence River, concluding with a quick run to Bermuda. There was also a two-week Christmas–New Year cruise to the Caribbean isles.

But faced with soaring operational costs, particularly from highly unionised, all-Swedish crews, coupled with highly increased fuel oil charges, Swedish American decided to pull out of the passenger ship business. In 1975, the 19-knot *Gripsholm* was withdrawn, laid up and offered for sale. Chandris Lines almost bought her, but instead she went to other Greeks,

During a long cruise to the Mediterranean and Black Sea, the 19-knot twin-screw *Gripsholm* is seen at Piraeus in Greece. (ALF collection)

Swedish American Line cruising 1961. (Author's collection)

the Karageorgis Lines, who renamed the 23,100-tonner as the *Navarino*. She ran Mediterranean cruises, often out of Venice, as well as some winter South American and even South African charter voyages.

She was sold again, however, and rather unexpectedly in the autumn of 1981. She was to have gone to Finnish buyers, the Sally Line, who wanted her for seven-day Miami–Caribbean service for their subsidiary Commodore Cruise Lines. Unfortunately, on 26 November, just as the sale documents were being finalised, she was in a floating dock at Skaramagas in Greece that capsized. The ship was flooded and declared a total loss – and so the deal was off. But salvage crews, including some former Swedish American Line officers and crew, put everything right again. Next, she passed to Italian investors, who renamed her *Samantha* and planned to run her on time-share Mediterranean cruises. Notably, she was the only liner then to be registered in Rome. But little else happened. She sat waiting at various anchorages.

In the autumn of 1985 she was sold yet again, this time to newly formed Regency Cruises. They refitted her as the *Regent Sea*. She sailed the Caribbean mostly, but also did Alaska cruises (from Vancouver) in high summer and occasionally made long cruises, such as seven weeks around South America. The Greek-owned Regency fleet continued to expand, acquiring such liners as the former *Statendam* and ex-*Shalom*. The eight-deck *Regent Sea* was, however, experiencing mechanical problems, which contributed to delayed and disrupted schedules. Later, there were food and water shortages as well. Her owners very abruptly declared bankruptcy in October 1995. Months later, the ship was to have set off from New York on a three-month trip around the world, the first such voyage for Regency. But, instead, poorly kept and rusting, the *Regent Sea* was initially sent to the Bahamas, to a backwater berth at Freeport, to escape a small army of creditors, bankers and even disgruntled passengers. Rumours abounded regarding her future. Among others, it was said that finally Commodore Cruise Lines would buy her or that Britain's Thomson Holidays would sail her as the *Topaz* (an assignment that later went to another veteran liner, the former *Carnivale* of Carnival Cruise Lines).

The much faded ship eventually went to auction for debts. Bought by so-called United States American Cruise Line and with her name shortened to *Sea*, she was moved but only to sit idle at Tampa, Florida, with reports of her being converted to a casino ship. But rather quickly, her new owners were bankrupt as well. Then the Swedish plan to buy her and bring her to Stockholm for use as a combination floating hotel and cruise terminal failed to materialise. Again, she went back to the auction block, but interested only Indian scrappers by this time.

13

SPAIN'S CABO LINERS: *CABO SAN ROQUE & CABO SAN VINCENTE (1957–59)*

When Seville-based Ybarra & Company, best known as the Ybarra Line, decided in the mid 1950s to build its two largest and finest passenger ships, they aroused additional attention by staging a national competition among young Spanish designers and decorators for what would be the largest ever Spanish passenger liners. The outcome was so pleasing, resulting in a high degree of modern rather than traditional or more customarily 'heavy' Spanish interior themes, that an exhibition devoted to the two new ships was sent on a tour not only within Spain, but to South America, where the ships would trade as well. Even the traditional design of two masts and two funnels was dropped and replaced by a single funnel with one mast placed above the bridge section. The ships would be named *Cabo San Roque* and *Cabo San Vicente*, and would be serious rivals to other South American-routed ships such as Italian Line's *Augustus* and *Giulio Cesare*, the French *Bretagne* and *Provence*, and Costa Line's brand-new *Federico C.*

Ordered from Sociedad Española de Construcción Naval at Bilbao, the *Cabo San Roque* was launched on 23 April 1955 and then completed in the late summer of 1957; the *Cabo San Vicente* went down the ways on 6 October 1956 and was delivered in April 1959. At nearly 15,000 tons, they used Sulzer diesels to reach top speeds of 22 knots if needed. The high-standard first-class quarters, with up to 241 berths, included separate public rooms, private bathrooms for all cabins and an outdoor lido deck with swimming pool. Tourist class, with 582 berths each, also had separate facilities, all cabins and no dormitories, and a separate lido and pool area. The ships were routed on a monthly service between Genoa, Barcelona, Palma de Mallorca, Cádiz, Lisbon and Tenerife, and then across to Rio de Janeiro, Santos, Montevideo and Buenos Aires. There was the occasion diversion. In 1965, the *Cabo San*

Vicente made, for example, a crossing to New York with Spanish tourists, students and entertainers for the World's Fair.

The sisters were also used for a considerable amount of cruising, particularly in the summer months during the peak of Spain's holiday trade. In the summer of 1967, for example, the 556ft-long *Cabo San Vicente* made a twenty-one-day cruise from Bilbao to Le Havre, Hamburg, Stockholm, Helsinki, Copenhagen, Bergen, Sognefjord, London, Le Havre and return

Summertime visitors: the *Cabo San Roque* (left) and the *Europa* seen together at Hamburg. (Author's collection)

to Bilbao. In that same summer, the *Cabo San Vicente* offered a fifteen-day voyage within the Mediterranean – from Barcelona to Genoa, Alexandria, Beirut, Haifa, Famagusta, Rhodes, Santorini, Genoa, Marseilles and return to Barcelona. A year later, in the summer of 1968, the same ship made two Mediterranean cruises, first from Barcelona to Cannes, Genoa, Capri, Messina, Piraeus, Varna, Constanza, Odessa, Yalta, Istanbul, Kusadasi, Messina, Capri, Genoa and return to Barcelona; the second, also from Barcelona, to Dubrovnik, Corfu, Istanbul, Yalta, Odessa, Constanza, Thasos, Mount Athos, Piraeus and Heraklion. Cruises were also run from South America, such as the two sailings of the *Cabo San Vicente* in the winter of 1968–69. The first voyage, lasting nearly two months, took the ship around continental South America – from Buenos Aires to Punta Arenas, Puerto Montt, Valparaiso, Callao, the Galapagos, Balboa, the Panama Canal, Kingston, Miami, St Thomas, Guadeloupe, Tobago, Trinidad, Bahia, Rio de Janeiro and Santos. Immediately after returning to Buenos Aires, she set off on a fifty-five-day run to Montevideo, Santos, Tenerife, Cádiz, Málaga, Barcelona, Palma de Mallorca, Dubrovnik, Istanbul, Constanza, Haifa, Piraeus, Naples, Livorno, Barcelona, Las Palmas and then a return to Santos and Rio de Janeiro.

By the early 1970s, despite the overall decline of traditional, two-class South American sailings, the two ships might have been refitted for more extensive cruising had it not been for the highly increased fuel oil costs of 1973–74. The *Cabo San Vicente* was offered for sale in the autumn of 1975 and went to the Mogul Line of India to become the pilgrim ship *Noor Jehan* for the Bombay–Jeddah trade. Eventually laid up in February 1984, she was subsequently broken up locally at Bombay. The *Cabo San Roque* was sold on a less happy occasion. Badly damaged by fire at a shipyard at Ferrol in Spain, on 24 January 1977, the damaged hulk was sold to Cypriot buyers, the Growth Maritime Investments Group, and towed to Piraeus for repairs. Renamed *Golden Moon*, there was some speculation that she would be rebuilt for the cruise trades, but this ended when, a year later, she was sold once again, this time to Fidel Castro's Cuban Government. Registered to Havana-based Empresa Navigación Mambisa, she was renamed *Africa Cuba* and fitted out as a troop transport and student ship. She was back on the mid-Atlantic route, but carrying far less jovial passengers than in her Ybarra days. Her time was limited, however. In the summer of 1982, in ill-kept, rusted condition and in need of considerable repairs, she was sold to Barcelona scrappers. Although Ybarra remained in the ferry trades for some years, they opted not to resume their liner operations after the *Cabo San Roque* and *Cabo San Vicente*.

14

REPARATIONS FOR ISRAEL: *JERUSALEM & THEODOR HERZL* (1957–58)

As I recall from watching ships, mostly passenger ships, at New York in the 1950s and '60s, the Zim Lines' *Jerusalem* and *Theodor Herzl* had somewhat peculiar movements. Beginning in 1959, the *Jerusalem* came each winter, making an Atlantic crossing from Haifa and other Mediterranean ports, for a three-month season of Caribbean cruises. She made the earliest of all morning departures, at 10 a.m. The *Theodor Herzl* came only once, dressed in flags, on a maiden crossing from Haifa. She was all but hidden, however, being berthed on the north side of Swedish American Line's Pier 97, at the very top end of Luxury Liner Row. Her white funnel barely poked above the pier shed.

The *Herzl* would go on to have a diverse old age. Despite the infirmities of old age, such as decreased economic efficiency which is often complicated by mechanical woes, shipowners sometimes see hope – and sometimes lots of

it – in second-hand passenger ships. Greek shipowners in particular once had a long track record in this area. Often, they could work wonders with older ships. An example was the case of the otherwise short-lived Fiesta Cruise Lines. They had high hopes for their 9,000-ton, 35-year-old *Fiesta*. She had been brought over from Florida and, once moored in Perama Bay near Piraeus, her resurrection began. She was to emerge as yet another 'new' cruise ship, taking travellers around the eastern Mediterranean in summers and in Caribbean waters in wintertime. But it all went astray when, on 24 October 1991, the 487ft-long ship caught fire, burned out and then, overloaded with firefighters' water, capsized. She was later righted and, in sections, cut up for scrap.

Clearly unknown to, say, the North American cruise industry as the *Fiesta*, the ship was perhaps better remembered as the Bermuda Star Line's

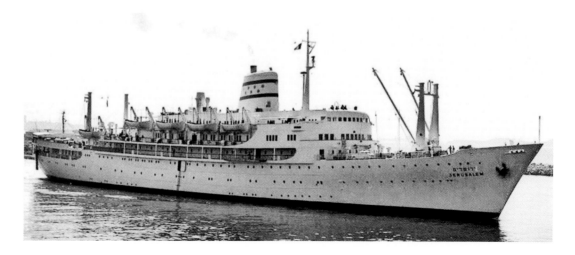

The 448ft-long *Jerusalem* and her sister were decorated by contemporary Israeli artists of the mid 1950s. (ALF collection)

Veracruz. Small by current standards and even somewhat out of step among this generation of high-tech mega cruise liners, the 'little *Veracruz*', as she was often called, was otherwise well known for her friendly ambience and her good travel value. She also had a rather interesting background.

Built at Hamburg in 1957, she was part of a four-passenger ship reparations pact between West Germany and Israel, namely the Zim Lines. First, there were the combination passenger-cargo type sisters *Israel* and *Zion*, created for the Haifa–Mediterranean–New York run. Then there were the sisters *Jerusalem* and *Theodor Herzl*. Together, they were the first brand-new Israeli passenger ships. The *Herzl* later became the *Veracruz* and then the *Fiesta*. Twin sisters, she and the *Jerusalem* were designed purposely for then busy inter-Mediterranean passenger trades, carrying immigrants, students and budget tourists mostly to and from Haifa on regular runs from Marseilles and Naples or sometimes from Venice. They each carried up to 560 passengers, all in tourist class. Young Israeli designers, decorators and artists did the interiors of the two ships. Along with the customary public rooms (including two dining rooms), each ship had a lower-deck cinema, an art gallery and a synagogue. There was a small pool and full sun deck aft. Most cabins were converted to daytime sitting rooms; some had private and others semi-private facilities. There were also some six-berth cabins as well as small dormitories for economy passages.

In winter, Zim Lines sent them cruising. The *Jerusalem* cruised from New York and later Port Everglades, Florida. The *Theodor Herzl*, named in honour of the founder of the Zionist movement, had at least one season operating between Los Angeles and the emerging Mexican Riviera. Later, she also made several immigrant crossings to and from South America, to Rio de Janeiro, Montevideo and Buenos Aires.

The gradual but later complete decline of migration by sea, alongside the excessively expensive maritime labour costs, prematurely ended the Zim careers of both ships. The *Jerusalem* went on, in 1966, to become the Florida-based cruise ship *Miami*, chartered to Miami-headquartered Peninsular & Occidental Steamship Company. But then rather quickly, within two years, in 1968, the charter was abruptly cancelled. Then the ship was sold outright to another Miami firm, the Eastern Steamship Lines. Renamed *New Bahama Star*, she was given a $5 million refit, modernised and was even fitted with the steam whistle from the original *Bahama Star*, a long-popular ship dating from 1931. Entering service in March 1969, the *New Bahama Star* was used in three- and four-day cruises between Miami and Nassau. Minimum fares for three nights began at $59 in 1969. While the name was changed to *Bahama Star* in 1972, she suffered boiler damage in October 1974, was laid up and then sold the following spring to Venezuelan buyers, who renamed her *Bonaire Star* with the intention of running Caribbean cruises. The project never materialised and the ship never sailed. Laid up at a Mobile, Alabama, shipyard, she was finally sold in April 1979 for $322,000 to New Orleans shipbreakers. Quickly, however, she was re-sold to German scrappers and then to Taiwanese scrap

During a Mediterranean cruise, the 9,914-ton *Theodor Herzl* is anchored at Valletta on Malta – with the Bulgarian-flag *Varna* on the left. (ALF collection)

merchants. Sadly, the empty ship sank in the Pacific while under tow for Kaohsiung on 3 October 1979.

The *Theodor Herzl*, withdrawn from Israeli service in 1970, was to become the *Carnivale* for the Arison Group, which would soon found Carnival Cruise Lines. Ted Arison, the founder, had strong ties to Israeli merchant shipping, which included Zim Lines, and had visions of a discount cruise line. The operation was affiliated with Boston-based ATS, the American Travel Service. She would have become the first Carnival Cruise Lines' ship, the beginning of an empire that, by 2015, owned fourteen cruise lines, running some 110 cruise ships. In fact, nothing came to pass and the ship was laid up, not sailing again for almost five years, until 1975. She was then refitted and re-commissioned for Miami–Nassau–Freeport cruising as the *Freeport* of Bahama Cruise Lines. She flew the Panamanian colours and was so altered that her capacity was increased to as much as 960. While her owners eventually changed their name to Bermuda Star Line, the ship itself went through a series of official name changes as well – first to *Veracruz I*, then to *Veracruz Primero* and finally to *Veracruz*. But then, after a varied cruising career that included Alaskan, Caribbean, Mexican and eastern Canada–New England itineraries, her sailing days ended.

15

STEAMING FOR RIO: *BRASIL & ARGENTINA* (1958)

'They were cosy, wonderful ships with special ambience,' recalled Captain Hans van Biljouw, when speaking of the Holland America Line sister ships *Veendam* and *Volendam*. He served aboard them, beginning in 1973, just as they were re-commissioned by their then new Dutch owners. Before that they had been US-flag liners, the *Argentina* and *Brasil* of Moore-McCormack Lines. The 617ft-long ships went on to have careers that lasted some forty-five years. 'Actually, I preferred the *Volendam*, the former *Brasil*,' added Captain van Biljouw. 'She had the better colours. She was darker, more coffee-like and therefore more Dutch in tone.'

Seen at Rio de Janeiro, the funnels aboard the 617ft-long *Argentina* and her sister were actually sun solariums. (Moore-McCormack Lines)

Arriving at New York for the first time, the *Brasil* and her sister cost an impressive $25 million each in 1958. (Moran Towing & Transportation Co.)

Completed in September and December 1958, the 15,200-ton sisters were the largest liners ever built in the American South, at the Ingalls shipyard at Pascagoula, Mississippi. Costing what was then a steep $25 million each, the 23-knot, twin-screw ships were designed for regular passenger as well as cruise services between New York and the east coast of South America. Their thirty-one-day round trips took them southward to Barbados or Trinidad, Rio de Janeiro, Santos, Montevideo and Buenos Aires. Minimum fare for the entire trip in the late 1950s was $1,110. They carried 553 passengers, all in first-class quarters, as well as three holds of cargo.

'They were excellent ships in most ways,' recalled the late Everett Viez, a passenger ship historian and photographer who made a South American cruise on the *Argentina*. 'They were noted, in travel circles, for their very

large cabins, perhaps the most spacious yet to go to sea. But they did not have especially attractive public rooms. The overall decor was too severely modern.'

Unfortunately, these twins were never very profitable under the stars and stripes. 'Actually, they should never have been built. Because of the airlines, it was too late for Latin American passenger service,' recalled a retired Moore-McCormack official. 'I remember that they were placed on "standby" by the US Government during the Cuban Missile Crisis in October 1962.'

The two liners were later sent more often on cruises – two weeks to the Caribbean from New York and Port Everglades, thirty-five days to Scandinavia and northern Europe in summer, and an annual long, luxury cruise in deep winter, such as sixty or so days to South America, across to Africa and then homeward via the Mediterranean.

Withdrawn from service in September 1969 after only eleven years of service under the US flag and laid up at the Maryland Shipbuilding & Drydock Company yard across from Baltimore, they were sold to Holland America two years later. 'The *Veendam* [ex-*Argentina*] and *Volendam* [ex-*Brasil*] were well-laid-out ships, especially in the crew areas,' recalled another Holland America officer, Captain Leo van Lanschot Hubrecht:

There was always much greater ease for the crew to do their jobs. But they were noted by us for their thick hull plating, which was created for possible

The 553-bed *Argentina*'s quarters included four suites and 182 staterooms. (Moore-McCormack Lines)

South America bound in advertising dated 1961. (Author's collection)

The *Brasil* and *Argentina* could also carry nearly 4,300 tons of cargo. (Alex Duncan)

Both ships were later rebuilt with a more box-like forward superstructure and modified funnels. To some, their original good looks were somewhat ruined. (Alex Duncan)

American military use. They were always 'well behaved', even in the worst weather. But they were difficult ships to manoeuvre. They did not have thrusters and, of course, were steam turbine, which made them more awkward. And they burned an extraordinary 120 tons of fuel per day. The *Nieuw Amsterdam* of 1983 burned 70 by comparison.

When fuel oil prices dramatically soared in 1973–74, the *Veendam* and *Volendam* were laid up at Newport News in Virginia. They remained together for almost a year, looked after by a crew of nine who lived ashore. There were plans to charter the *Veendam* (ex-*Argentina*) to New York-based Flagship Cruises, which had just sold off their *Sea Venture* and *Island Venture* to Princess Cruises, and sail her as the *Sea Venture II*. Then another charter was considered. Wall Street Cruises, also with headquarters in Manhattan, were interested in running the *Veendam* as the *Constitution* on two- and five-day cruises of New York. In December 1974, the same ship finally found a firm, five-month charter to a Brazilian company, who sailed her as the *Brasil*. Thus, the former *Argentina* sailed as the *Brasil*!

In the summer of 1975, both ships were chartered to Miami-based, Greek-owned, Panama-flagged Monarch Cruise Lines. The *Veendam* became the *Monarch Star*, while the *Volendam* changed to *Monarch Sun*. In 1978, they rejoined Holland America and reverted to their Holland America names. They were sold off in 1983–84, just as the sisters *Nieuw Amsterdam* and *Noordam* came into service. Ownership and frequent name changes coloured their subsequent histories: the *Veendam* (ex-*Argentina)* became the *Bermuda Star*, *Enchanted Isle*, *Commodore Hotel* and then back to *Enchanted Isle*. The *Volendam* (ex-*Brasil*) changed to *Island Sun*, *Liberté*, *Canada Star*, *Queen of Bermuda*, *Enchanted Seas* and, by 1996, to *Universe Explorer*.

The author cruised aboard the *Liberté* in July 1986, on one of her short-lived seven-day cruises out of Papeete in Tahiti. Run by an arm of C.Y. Tung's American Hawaii Cruises, even the discounted passage fares coupled with the $199 air add-on from the US east coast were not adequate to convince enough passengers to fill the 600-plus berths. Furthermore, the entire operation was foiled by problems with local French officials.

Almost typically, the two aged ships ended their days at the hands of Indian shipbreakers. The former *Argentina*, under the temporary name *New Orleans*, was delivered to the scrap crews in December 2003; the ex-*Brasil* followed a year later, in December 2004.

COSTA LINE NEW BUILD (1958)

Within ten years of its first passenger sailings aboard rebuilt ships, including austere, migrant-carrying ex-freighters, Italy's Costa Line introduced not only their first brand-new liner, but one of the finest – and some added most handsome – Italian liners of the 1950s. Company directors turned to a local shipyard, Ansaldo at Genoa, who proudly displayed the designs they had used for the splendid *Andrea Doria* and *Cristoforo Colombo* just a few years before and also for the forthcoming *Leonardo da Vinci*, which would be ready by 1960. The new Costa flagship would be something of a 'distant cousin' to these ships. She was launched on 31 March 1957 as the *Federico C*.

The new ship, at 20,400 tons and with a capacity for 1,279 passengers in three classes, was immediately acclaimed as one of the finest ships of her time. Just after her maiden voyage from Genoa – on her regular run to Cannes, Barcelona, Lisbon and then across to Rio de Janeiro, Santos, Montevideo and Buenos Aires – in March 1958, she was also said to be the finest Italian liner on the Latin American run. Completely air conditioned and stabilised, her level of decor (even in third class) was appraised as 'stunning contemporary'. She even surpassed, according to some, Italian Line's larger *Augustus* and *Giulio Cesare* on that same South Atlantic service. The accommodation aboard the 21-knot *Federico C* had at least five public rooms for each class, pools and lido decks for each, and all first-class and many second-class cabins had private facilities. And, of course, she proudly upheld the high standards that had become well known about Costa's kitchens and level of service. The new ship had one blemish: stability problems. 'Like the subsequent *Leonardo da Vinci*, the *Federico C* had to be specially fitted with concrete ballast,' reported Maurizio Eliseo, one of the foremost Italian maritime historians and authors.

The 606ft-long *Federico C* was joined in South American service by the smaller, converted *Anna C* and *Andrea C*. Costa were so impressed with their new flagship that they soon began to plan for a larger, faster, more luxurious version. This ship would be, of course, the 30,000-ton, 1,600-passenger *Eugenio C*, completed eight years later, in 1966.

By 1968, however, the South American liner trade, both for first-class clientele and the once overflowing migrant trade in third class, was in decline. The airlines had arrived – and in a powerful, decisive way. The *Federico C* was moved over to the Genoa–Caribbean service, which included transatlantic service to and from Port Everglades, Florida, to Madeira, Lisbon, Barcelona, Cannes, Genoa and Naples. But soon this too slowed and gave way to full-time cruising – in the Caribbean, the Mediterranean and in South America (from Rio, Santos and Buenos Aires). She also made Costa's annual month-long August holiday cruise as well, an itinerary that took her to Scandinavia and northern Europe.

In 1983, Costa – then restyled as Costa Cruises – decided to reorganise and modernise its fleet, which was then the largest apart from the Soviet

Italian beauty: the good looks of the 20,416grt 606ft-long *Federico C* were based to some extent on the *Andrea Doria* and *Cristoforo Colombo*. (ALF collection)

passenger ship fleet. They also decided to trim their fleet and so, among other dispositions, they sold the 25-year-old *Federico C* to Florida-based Premier Cruise Lines. Premier wanted a ship for twice-weekly three- and four-day cruises from Port Canaveral to the Bahamas that could be directly linked to their busy tour business with nearby Disney World. In fact, through a marketing arrangement, Premier Cruise Lines was soon also known as 'the Mickey Mouse cruise line'. Renamed *Royale*, the ex-Costa flagship was refitted (which included repainting the hull in bright red). She entered service in February 1984. In less than two years, success was at hand and she was joined by another Italian-built liner, Home Lines' brilliant former *Oceanic*. Although not actually renamed, the two liners were advertised as the *Starship Royale* and *Starship Oceanic*. But once Premier bought another former Home Lines cruise ship, the *Atlantic*, the older, smaller *Royale* was back on the sales lists.

In February 1989, she hoisted the colours of Greek-owned Dolphin Cruise Lines (she was, in fact, registered to Panama-flag owners called Ulysses Cruises) and was renamed *Sea Breeze I* for seven-day Miami–Caribbean cruise service. She later made alternative cruises. The author was on board in June 1999 when she sailed from Philadelphia on a two-night cruise 'to nowhere'. But, most unusually, she 'poked' into New York Harbor on the first morning, sailed along the lower Hudson River, went north and passed under the George Washington Bridge, turned, reversed course and left the harbour just after lunch. A hundred members of the Steamship Historical Society of America were aboard and I did the narrative broadcast to the outer decks and public rooms of New York Harbor history, landmarks and notations.

Dolphin later fell into deep financial trouble, was acquired by Premier in 1997 and so the *Sea Breeze I* returned to her previous owners. But then Premier itself collapsed in September 2000 and, to avoid being 'arrested' for debt, the *Sea Breeze I* all but dumped her final passengers at Halifax and was laid up in that Nova Scotia port. But then, three months later, in December, while supposedly fleeing to foreign waters (the Bahamas), she sank – reportedly under 'mysterious circumstances' – off the American east coast. An alternative report was that she had in fact been bought by a holding company, Cruise Ventures, and was bound for a shipyard at Charleston, South Carolina. But in storm-tossed seas off the Virginia coast, her boilers allegedly broke, created a hole in the ship's side and she began to flood. Her small crew of thirty-four was rescued using helicopters by the US Coast Guard. Quietly, the former *Federico C* slipped under the waves. A subsequent investigation revealed that the 42-year-old liner was worth $5–6 million in scrap, but was insured for $20 million. Because the ship flew the Panamanian flag and was too far off the Virginia coast, and therefore out of US legal domain, no full investigation of the sinking was ever done.

Italian trio: the *Federico C*, *Augustus* and *Cristoforo Colombo* at Genoa – and all berthed in 'stern-in' style. (Richard Faber collection)

Progression: the great success of the *Federico C* led to the larger, improved, more luxurious *Eugenio C*, completed eight years later, in 1966. (Costa Line)

17

INNOVATIVE DUTCH FLAGSHIP: THE SPLENDID *ROTTERDAM* (1959)

The 1950s were indeed a golden, albeit final, era for ocean liners. Each year of the decade, it seemed, produced great passenger ships, flagships and 'ships of state'. As the decade drew to a close, interest and the future seemed bright – airline competition was not yet fully noticed or threatening. The French, for example, were building the 66,000-ton *France*, Cunard talked of a 75,000-ton replacement for the ageing *Queen Mary* and the Italians were creating a replacement for the sunken *Andrea Doria*. The West Germans added two splendidly converted liners, the *Hanseatic* and *Bremen*. Even the Spanish were thinking of a pair of 20,000-tonners for transatlantic service. American Export Lines still hoped for a third big liner, Canadian Pacific ordered a third *Empress* liner and all while Holland America planned for its biggest liner yet. The Dutch had long wanted a serious running mate to the glorious *Nieuw Amsterdam*, which had turned 20 in 1958.

The new flagship, ordered in 1956, would come from the Rotterdam Drydock Company yard at Rotterdam. Locally designed and built, she would be a Dutch ship from end to end, the flagship of the still-mighty Dutch Merchant Marine. Her design was kept a secret, however. She would be different – she would not have traditional funnels, but instead twin uptakes awhich would be placed aft. As one company master recalled, 'We were amazed at first – there were no smokestacks!'

Like her mother before her, in the case of the *Nieuw Amsterdam* (in April 1937), Her Majesty Queen Juliana named the new flagship at launching ceremonies on 13 September 1958. The *Rotterdam*, at 38,645 tons, would be slightly larger than the *Nieuw Amsterdam*, but 10ft shorter. A year later, during the maiden crossing from Rotterdam to New York, Crown Princess Beatrix was aboard to commemorate the occasion. The princess disembarked in the Lower Bay and then landed at Pier A in Lower Manhattan, prior to attending a welcoming ticker-tape parade along Lower Broadway, which included passing the Holland America Line offices at 29 Broadway. Later, after docking at the company's terminal at the foot of 5th Street in Hoboken, the 748ft-long *Rotterdam* was shifted across the lower Hudson to Pier 40, at West Houston Street in Greenwich Village. While far from complete, Pier 40 would be the innovative new home of the Holland America Line.

Journalist and maritime historian Frank Braynard attended a welcome luncheon aboard the sparklingly new Dutch flagship. He later recalled, 'The

The classic-looking inbound *Nieuw Amsterdam* passes the incomplete *Rotterdam*, just prior to launching in a photo dated 13 September 1958. (Holland America Line)

The 748ft *Rotterdam* fitting out at the Rotterdam Dry Dock yard in the summer of 1959. (Holland America Line)

Maiden arrival of the splendid *Rotterdam* in New York's Upper Bay in September 1959. (Holland America Line)

Rotterdam was nothing short of stunning as well as innovative. She was the beginning, we thought and we later wrote, of a new ocean liner age. Myself, I found the lack of smokestacks to be different, innovative and quite brave of Holland America. From stem to stern, she was an absolutely gorgeous ship!' Among her thirteen passenger decks were over fifteen public rooms, indoor and outdoor swimming pools, and the largest movie theatre then afloat, seating 607 in all.

Sailing every Friday at noon, from April through October, the three big Holland America liners – *Nieuw Amsterdam*, *Statendam* and *Rotterdam* – sailed from Hoboken for Southampton, Le Havre and Rotterdam. Like the other two liners, the *Rotterdam* was intentionally designed for alternative winter cruising, taking only up to 730 one-class passengers (her normally capacity was 1,456 in two classes). In December 1959, beginning her first winter season, the *Rotterdam* undertook her first long cruises – forty-nine days around South America followed by seventy-five nights to South America, Africa and Europe. Fares for the latter began at $2,400 or $32 per person per day. She began making an annual around-the-world cruise, for approximately ninety days in duration, beginning a year later, in January 1961. In January 1983, she

The 1,456-passenger *Rotterdam* arrives at Hoboken, just off the American Export Lines' terminal. The radiantly new and innovative Dutch flagship had cost £13 million to construct. (Holland America Line)

Another view, also from 1959, of Holland's two most beloved liners. (Holland America Line)

Holland's largest and grandest liners, the *Rotterdam* and *Nieuw Amsterdam*, swap berths at the 5th Street pier in Hoboken. This view dates from December 1959. (Flying Camera Inc.)

set off on the company's Silver Jubilee World Cruise. By then, fares started at $15,000.

The *Rotterdam* had an immensely successful career and attracted armies of loyal followers. Some passengers came year after year – and this included many repeaters on the world cruises. Carnival Cruise Lines bought Holland America in 1989, but retained the ageing *Rotterdam* for another seven years, until September 1997. Carnival was not interested, it seemed, in giving the liner a $40 million refit it needed to meet new, stricter safety standards. The *Rotterdam* made her farewell Holland America cruise beginning on 30 September 1997. Some of her fittings were sold off during the voyage, nostalgic souvenirs to loyalist passengers.

Quickly sold to Premier Cruises and renamed *Rembrandt*, she was soon refitted, hereafter met the upgraded safety standards and began weekly cruises from Port Canaveral, Florida. She sailed with several well-known ocean liners – namely the former *Oceanic*, *Eugenio C* and *Transvaal Castle* – that belonged to Premier. Premier was increasingly over-extended, however, and on 13 September 2000 the company shut down. The *Rembrandt* was ordered to offload her passengers and some crew at Halifax and then proceed to Freeport in the Bahamas to be laid up.

Right. Early world cruising on the *Rotterdam*. (Author's collection)

Far right. Crossing to and from Europe – 'It's good to be on a well-run ship,' according to Holland America. (Author's collection)

All while baking in the Bahamian sun and with scant maintenance and care, the *Rembrandt* remained at Freeport for almost four years. She might have been sold for scrap but nostalgic Dutch investors bought her and, on 12 July 2004, the neglected ship arrived under tow at Gibraltar for the removal of asbestos. Restoration followed at shipyards in Spain, Poland and Germany until she returned to home waters, to Rotterdam, on 8 August 2008. Renamed *Rotterdam* and repainted in her original late 1950s colouring, she opened to the public on 15 February 2010 as a combination museum, hotel, entertainment complex and vocational training school. Her future was, however, troubled. There were huge financial overruns, debt and weak revenues. Rumours circulated that she would be sold, heading for a Middle Eastern port for use as a conference centre. Instead, in June 2013, the *Rotterdam* was sold to WestCord Hotels, which also owned the nearby Hotel New York, located in the former Holland America Line headquarters at the Wilhelminakade in Rotterdam. Superbly restored and outfitted, the *Rotterdam* remains in home waters – a testament to the great liners of the 1950s.

18

ANOTHER ITALIAN BEAUTY: *LEONARDO DA VINCI (1960)*

Shortly after the *Andrea Doria* went to the bottom on a summer's morning in 1956, Italian Line designers and engineers began work on a replacement. In the still very busy Atlantic passenger trade, there was a huge gap in the company's services, especially on its express run between Naples, Genoa, Cannes, Gibraltar and New York. Normally on the South American run, the sisters *Augustus* and *Giulio Cesare* and even the veteran *Conte Grande* made extra trips on the northern run to New York. The *Cristoforo Colombo*, the *Doria*'s sister, advanced to the role of national flagship, at least for a time. The new ship, as suggested by the Genoa-based directors and government benefactors in Rome, had to be an improvement: bigger, faster, more lavish.

In December 1959, on one of our Saturday outings in and around Manhattan, my grandfather and I stopped in at Grand Central Terminal, the grand railway terminal on East 42nd Street. An 18ft-long model of the new Italian Line flagship was on display. Glass-encased and specially lighted, she seemed a modern, sleek design, equal to the superb exterior of the 29,000-ton *Andrea Doria* and *Cristoforo Colombo*. That model of the 33,500-ton *Leonardo da Vinci* has somehow remained a vivid memory, one of those hooks in the mental department of long-ago events. I did not expect to see that model ever again. But in August 2001, during a visit to Monte Carlo, there it was – a second sighting, a fresh encounter, another memorable occasion.

While the 760ft-long ship itself arrived for the first time at New York's Pier 84 on a humid morning in July 1960, I was almost hypnotically watching from the Hoboken shore. The new liner was stunningly beautiful. The model itself had long since returned to Italy and to Italian Line headquarters at Genoa. There were, in fact, slight differences compared to the actual ship – changes no doubt made in the final stages of construction such as modifications to the funnel and to the forward superstructure. The

model had made, nevertheless, a splendid recreation. The 1,326-passenger *da Vinci* went on to sail in both Mediterranean and cruise service before the Italian Line, or actually the Italian Government, which paid all the bills, pulled the highly subsidised plug in 1975–76. Even the newer, larger and more luxurious sisters *Michelangelo* and *Raffaello* were relegated to lay-up and then later sold to the Iranian Government for use as floating army barracks in quiet Middle Eastern backwaters. The 23-knot *da Vinci* actually made the last Italian Line crossing in June 1976. Afterward, she was sent cruising full time (for newly created Italian Line Cruises International and with Costa Line management), but with little success. Among other dilemmas, she had early stability problems, for this she had to be loaded with cement which altogether caused her to be hard on fuel. She was very expensive to run, even when filled to capacity. Finally, she was laid up and then sold for scrap. But on the eve of her demolition at La Spezia, a fire mysteriously erupted,

Comparisons: the 29,000grt *Cristoforo Colombo* and, slightly larger, the 33,000grt *Leonardo da Vinci*. (Italian Line)

A Saturday morning gathering at New York in June 1975 – the *Statendam* (top), then the *Rotterdam, Oceanic, Michelangelo, Doric* and the bow of the *Sagafjord*. (Port Authority of New York & New Jersey)

LEAN BACK and relax to Europe. The tower will still be standing long after your glorious vacation voyage on

Italian Line Battery Pk.Bldg.
24 State St., New York 4
Tel. Digby 4-0800
See your TRAVEL AGENT

Crossing on the Italian Line, 1961. (Author's collection)

Night-time at Genoa: the *Rhodesia Castle,* the freighter *President Jackson* and the mighty *Leonardo da Vinci.* (ALF collection)

The 761ft-long *Leonardo da Vinci* enters dry dock at Genoa for final outfitting in June 1960. (Italian Line)

It was rumoured in the early 1960s that the steam turbine-driven *Leonardo da Vinci* would be converted to nuclear propulsion in 1965. (ALF collection)

Burning to death at La Spezia on 4 July 1980. (Antonio Scrimali)

Goddess in ruins: the capsized *da Vinci*. (Antonio Scrimali)

destroyed much of the ship and then – overloaded with firefighters' water – she capsized on 4 July 1980. Her charred remains were later salvaged before being broken up.

The model remained with the Italian Line until their grand Genoa head office was closed in 1977. Later, it passed into private hands, to Maurizio Eliseo, one of Italy's foremost maritime historians and authors. Stored for a time in a garage near Milan, the intricate detailing grew faded, dusty, even damaged. Model restoration is, of course, a skilled and costly business. But by the late 1990s, with enough monies in hand, Eliseo struck a deal with some Russian model makers in St Petersburg, all of them formerly employed by the Soviet Navy. Stowed on a large flatbed truck, the model set off across central Europe and then northward to the Baltic. The resulting restoration was nothing short of idyllic, right down to miniature umbrella-topped tables set around the three swimming pools and deckchairs placed just behind the long rows of Promenade Deck windows. Freshly repainted, re-rigged from end to end, and with each and every lifeboat, railing and piece of deck equipment in place, the model returned to Italy in the spring of 2001 and then was loaned to the Monaco Maritime Museum. Just as I remember from Grand Central all those years before, it sat in glowing, lighted perfection. It is a glorious reminder of the beautiful *Leonardo da Vinci* – and the great passenger liners of the 1950s.

BIBLIOGRAPHY

Braynard, Frank O. & Miller, William H., *Picture History of the Cunard Line 1840–1990* (Dover Publications, 1991)

Kludas, Arnold, *Great Passenger Ships of the World*, Vol. II (Patrick Stephens Wellingborough, 1984)

—, *Great Passenger Ships of the World*, Vol. III ((Patrick Stephens Wellingborough, 1984)

Miller, William H., *Going Dutch: The Holland America Line Story* (Carmania Press, 1998)

—, *Great British Passenger Ships* (The History Press, 2010)

—, *Pictorial Encyclopaedia of Ocean Liners, 1860–31994* (Dover Publications, 1991)

—, *Picture History of British Ocean Liners, 1900 to the Present* (Dover Publications, 2001)

—, *Picture History of German and Dutch Passenger Ships* (Dover Publications, 2001)

—, *Picture History of the French Line* (Dover Publications, 1997)

—, *Picture History of the Italian Line, 1932–1977* (Dover Publications, 1999)

—, *The First Great Ocean Liners in Photographs 1897–1927* (Dover Publications, 1984)